DUANE ARTHUR OSE

ALASKAN
ADVENTURE I

JOIN DUANE AND HIS SON DANIEL ON A JOURNEY DEEP IN THE ALASKAN WILDERNESS IN SEARCH OF FINDING A NEW HOME

www.osemountainalaska.com

STRATTON
—PRESS—
Publishing Life

ALASKAN WILDERNESS ADVENTURE
Copyright © 2019 **Duane Arthur Ose**

Stratton Press Publishing
831 N Tatnall Street Suite M #188,
Wilmington, DE 19801
www.stratton-press.com
1-888-323-7009

ISBN (Paperback): 978-1-64345-672-0
ISBN (Ebook): 978-1-64345-838-0

Printed in the United States of America

This book is dedicated to my mother, Adora May Ose,
age ninety-three, who brought me into this world.
Love you, Mom.

CONTENTS

PREFACE

November 17, 1977, was the day I caught a .22 caliber long rifle bullet in my head. The bullet entered through the left lens of my eyeglasses. It struck my upper eyelid, destroying my eye. Zipping on, the bullet made its way to the back of my brain, hugging the left inner wall of my skull. The metal slug plowed up a trail of bone fragments, as though it was the Grim Reaper scything a trail to my grave.

Deflecting off the back of my skull, the bullet went behind my cerebellum (the small part of the brain located on top of the brain stem), and that is where the bullet came to its final resting spot, embedded in the center of the right half of my brain. In its race to end my life, the bullet didn't escape unscathed. It was fragmented into two pieces and resides in my brain to this day.

The human body is an amazing thing. My body formed a natural growth around the bullet. This growth encased the bullet, preventing my body from absorbing the lead, which could have resulted in lead poisoning. The doctors deemed it inoperable. It would be too risky to attempt a removal operation.

There is much more to tell regarding my brain injury, but I'm saving that to be shared in another book. The story you are about to discover takes place during the time in my life when I was newly in love with Alaska and the wilderness she wears. I made it my mission to stake a claim on this land I love, and I became the last person to file for a federal homestead in the United States of America, making history.

I was conscious from the time I was shot, until I was laying on an operating table in the Willmar, Minnesota, hospital. While on an ice-cold operating table, only able to see out of one eye, I was looking up at the bright lights, and the operating team circled around me. The doctors and other staff could do no more than stop the bleeding and stabilize me.

The doctor said to me, "We have to remove your eye, so we will put you to sleep. You are in good hands now."

"Dear Lord, my life is in your hands."

The next instant, I found myself outside in the cold winter air. I looked about, trying to figure out where I was. I could see the hospital to my left, a few blocks away. I was standing on a sidewalk, looking across the street. Lining the sidewalks were intervals of decorative green lamp posts. The lamps were pointed on the top, each with a soft glowing bulb, which didn't offer much illumination. There was snow piled at the bases of the buildings around me. I noticed the snow had been shoveled by someone using a handheld snow shovel. Little details that I shall never forget.

I was standing there alone; I couldn't see anyone around me. There was an alley across the street from where I stood, to my left. There were buildings made of brick on each side of the narrow alley.

An old man emerged from the alleyway and made his way toward me. As he reached the center of the street, I could see that he was in need. I said to myself, "This man needs my help. Whatever he asks of me, I will give."

Up until that moment, I had been freezing cold, dressed with only my shirt and pants on. As this man came closer, I became blessedly warm.

The man was dressed in a blue Sunday suit, clothing that clearly weren't his. They were far too large and baggy. He wore a dress hat, on which there was a band circling around it, with a bow on the side. His hat was pulled down tight on his head, bending his ears outward. He stood with his hands in his pockets. His face was unshaven, having inch-long whiskers standing stiffly from his face. He must not have shaved for weeks.

He stepped up on the curb and pressed his right side against me to share in my warmth. While he was close at my side, I grew even warmer. I was taller than he was, but being this close, I could see his eyes were meridian green. When he spoke to me, it was with a Norwegian accent. "Have you any cold, cold cash on you?"

"Gee, I'm terribly, terribly sorry. But you see, I don't have a dime on me." I reached my arm out and pointed to the hospital. "The hospital has all my money locked up."

With that said, he walked back toward the alleyway he had come out of. When he reached the center of the street, a bright, glowing light absorbed him. He was gone. The light traveled toward me, growing so bright I couldn't see myself, or him, or anything. The light had absorbed me as well.

The next thing I knew, I found myself standing in a garden on a path. I could see an archway ahead, so I followed the path up to it. A man dressed in a robe walked up to me from this arch holding his hands up, palms facing toward me. "It is not yet your time." I could see behind him there were people beyond that arch.

Suddenly, I woke up. I was in the recovery room. I knew at that moment what had just transpired was a test on my character, and I had passed. If I hadn't passed, I would have gone straight to hell that day. Of this, I am certain.

There was a very important lesson instilled in me from this experience: no matter how bad a person's life might seem, others have it worse. Live by example. Always push yourself to do better. Set your goals high, and push yourself to achieve the best life you can. I took a vow to enjoy the rest of my life.

The wounds I received from being shot were disabling, causing difficult problems to contend with—enough problems to keep me from qualifying for gainful employment. I didn't want to live on welfare, and the insurance money I had coming in wouldn't last forever. The wounds I incurred would greatly affect my income and lifestyle.

Five years went by. At some point during that time, my wife and I divorced, sharing our three children with joint custody. These were not good times for any of us. It wasn't horrible, but it could have been much better. We still had our good moments, our family times.

My father, Clarence, died one night from a massive heart attack. In the months following his death, I was asked to ride up to Alaska with one of my second cousins, Mike E. Ose of Wasilla, Alaska. He made a deal with me; I would spend the summer in Alaska, then Mickey would buy me a plane ticket to fly back to Minnesota come fall.

Mickey showed me around, and I explored some of the Alaskan country on my own. My interests were not in the urban areas or places where road systems were found. I'm a country boy at heart; my interest was in the wilderness.

The next year, 1984, my oldest son, David, and I set out for Alaska. It was a 3,500-mile drive from Granite Falls, Minnesota, up to Alaska. We arrived in Wasilla, Alaska, where we would be staying with Mickey while helping him build his log home.

It was during my stay with Mickey that I learned about the homesteading opportunity in Alaska. There were two areas open for settlement, both of thirty thousand acres in size. I armed myself fully with all the information, charts, and rules. I also procured a black and white large photo, which had been taken from space of the Lake Minchumina Land Settlement Area. I chose to search for land in this area, rather than the Solana District, simply because the other was located too close to civilization. I had to explore it firsthand to be sure.

Armed with all the information we would need to pursue the homesteading dream, Dave and I drove back to Granite Falls. We stopped for a Dairy Queen treat before traveling the final thirteen miles to Wood Lake, Minnesota.

I saw my chance to live within my means, to take part of the Homestead Act of 1862. An act that would come to a close October of 1986, never to reopen again.

My first step was to visit this new land, to see the land in person before I would decide whether or not it was meant for me. This could be the last stand in my life. My last hope to be self-sustaining, rather than depending on others. My final opportunity to be a landowner while I was still young. My final chance to live. This brings us to the start of my *Alaskan Wilderness Adventure*.

CHAPTER ONE

To Be or Not To Be, 1984

While visiting family in Anchorage and Wasilla, I gained many new friends from all over Alaska. I was hungry for their input. I wanted to know their likes and dislikes pertaining to Alaskan living. I wanted opinions from both genders and all ages.

The only complaint I heard came from the women. None of them complained about the cold winters; they had warm clothing for solving that issue. It was the long, dark winter nights they complained of. Having no sun at all, or very little. To help deal with the lack of sun, Alaskans have plenty of bright lighting. They also take tablets to make sure they have sufficient vitamin D.

Alaska is where women sleep all winter and stay awake partying during the long daylight hours of summer.

During the days of my childhood, I learned to explore the land on foot. I started from my backyard, moving bravely outward, experiencing the land firsthand. I was younger then, but I did this once again while visiting Alaska. Unlike Minnesota, here I could find total and complete wilderness, untouched by man. A different plant life and a different habitat. The weather was very different as well due to the difference in elevations.

I will always have a love for my birthplace, the Minnesota River Valley, but a new land of adventure was beckoning me. I was not interested in renting or owning a small portion of property, and that was all I could afford in Minnesota. I saw the last frontier on earth, Alaska, and knew I could make a new life there—having the freedom to breathe, to make a new life free from restrictions of movement, to feel like I was no longer tethered.

A person can be free in Minnesota as well, but I was not ready for a rocking chair. That would have been my fate, had I stayed in Minnesota. For having a profitable job was not an option. I had the foresight to know I would quickly get bored staying in Minnesota. Out in Alaska, I could live remotely surviving on my fixed income and living off the land. In Alaska, I could build my own house, trap fur for extra income, and hunt and fish for food resources.

I had to take the first steps in making my dreamland come true. I had to find the piece of land I wanted to own and live on so that I could stake my claim.

I looked at the land areas for sale in Alaska, but they were all so close to the urban areas, I knew I would be surrounded by others in a short time. I could clearly see the future of expansion into the rural areas. It would not be for me in the long term. It's not that I dislike people, but for my plans, I needed room.

One day, a friend informed me that there were two federal land areas open for homesteading. The very next day, I found my way into the federal land office in Anchorage, the Bureau of Land Management (BLM). I told the woman working at the reception desk that I was interested in learning more about claiming a federal homestead. I picked up every folder, brochure, and form they had pertaining to filing for a homestead.

In order to stake a claim, I had to bring with me a staking application. This packet contained the forms for applying for a homestead. It also included the rules that applied and the conditions that I needed to fulfill in order to qualify for a homestead claim.

I left the office and headed back to Mickey Ose's place, the Carefree Acres. His property was located outside of the town of Wasilla. At that time, Wasilla was a small, growing town. Mickey was the owner of five acres of wooded, undeveloped land in that subdivision. His property was modest. There was not much more than a bulldozed driveway, a small one-car garage, and a twenty-foot Indian lodge, also known as a tepee.

The lodge was brought up from Minnesota in 1982, by Mickey and me. David, my eldest son, came up with me during that trip. He was fifteen years old at that time. We lived in that lodge while David and I built Mickey's log cabin, using the trees on his land. The cabin David and I built is now located at the center of Mickey's finished house. It was a first-time experience for Dave and me, using logs to build a structure.

Mickey was a skilled pipe fitter, making good money working on the northern slope of Alaska. While putting in overtime every month, he sent back a large check, which I deposited into his bank account. Up on the slope, there was no need for money, as there were no expenses. It was a working camp, where the oil company provided transportation to and from work, as well as providing all the needs of the workers on the slope. (There is more to this story, to be told in another book.)

When David and I weren't busy building the cabin, I soaked in the information on the Federal Homestead Act. The Federal Homestead Act was first opened in 1862, to be closed for good in October of 1986. This act leads to the flourishing growth and expansion of the western frontier. The Homestead Act opened doors to new land in undeveloped country. It gave an opportunity for people, like me, to prosper. Most people that tried to stake a claim ended up losing their land from not meeting the requirements.

There are two areas that were opened for homesteaders to stake a claim. The first settlement area is called the Solana District. It looked nice, had big trees that would have come in handy for building a home, but it was blocked from public access by eleven miles of native territory. Permission would have been needed to access the Solana District, by passing through the native lands. I did not want to be reliant on the cooperation of total strangers. Plus, it was not far enough from people.

The Solana District might have been just right for some, but not for me. The next chance I had, I went back to the BLM office and purchased a high-altitude black and white photo of the second land area open for homesteaders—the Lake Minchumina Land Settlement Area.

I purchased land topographic maps as well. I needed these in order to assist in my overland trek, starting our hike at Lake Minchumina. There were lakes to land a plane on in this land opening, but I wanted to get to know the land by exploring. I wanted a firsthand view of the location. I needed to see the lay of the land so I could study it. I wanted to get the total feel for the land, much like a sodbuster farmer would do when laying claim for their land, way back in the early years of homesteading.

There were sixty-four claims filed as soon as the Lake Minchumina area opened up for homesteaders. Most of the land was claimed the same day of the opening, in December of 1982. All the best shorelines were claimed on the five tundra ponds, which bore no official names. These ponds were too shallow to be worth anything, or dependable for resources. All they were good for was serving as a mosquito habitat; mosquitoes love the lowlands. Being of Norwegian descent, I loved the hills. A good lake would have been nice, but in this settlement area, there were no decent lakes.

Permafrost is prevalent in all lowlands, including areas sheltered from the sun in this district. (Permafrost runs one thousand feet deep.) Building on stilts was not an option for me. I wanted a high country hillside facing the sun. I wanted a place overlooking the tundra ponds and swamps. No, my plans were not to get off a plane and hastily build something that would not last. I didn't want to settle for an area lacking a panoramic view of the McKinley mountain range. Besides, it would be cold in the bottom land. Cold sinks, don't yah know?

Mike Houseman, a good friend of mine from Willmar, made arrangements to fly up and spend a few months with us. He would help drive back down the Alaskan Canadian Highway once we completed our mission for this trip.

Through teamwork, David and I were able to complete our work on Mickey's log cabin before the snow set in. We didn't leave in time for Dave to start his school year in Wood Lake. David had enrolled in Wasilla High School until we were ready to drive the

3,500 miles back home. Once we were done with our tasks, we made that trip in a record time of three days. We only stopped to eat, fuel up, and stretch our legs. Traveling on this highway in early fall is not wise due to unpredictable weather conditions. It was a race to get back home for more than one reason. The main thing was to get David back in school.

CHAPTER TWO

Be Prepared

During the spring of 1985, my youngest son, Daniel, and I were planning for our drive up to Alaska from Minnesota. We needed to prepare for the arduous hike that would be facing us. Soon after the school year ended, we loaded our camping supplies.

There was a long list of supplies to make sure we were amply prepared: a four-man Eureka tent, sleeping bags, an internal frame mountain backpack, an external frame mountain backpack, a tube container for rolled up maps, topographical maps, the black-and-white photo of the settlement area, charts, a folding grill, a frying pan, cooking oil, lightweight camp kettles, metal plates, eating utensils, waterproof matches, spices, bars of soap, toothpaste, toothbrushes, towels, washcloths, toilet paper, extra changes of clothing, leather gloves, hats, a box of Pic coils (this item kills mosquitoes), rain gear, a roll of duct tape, a large section of clear poly sheeting, 100 feet of 1/2-inch rope, a journal, two pens, a 35mm camera, film, a Mossberg short barrel .22 rifle, 500 rounds of .22 caliber long rifle bullets, a white metal detector, two three-foot gas welder's rods of 1/8 inch diameter (for dowsing), two pocket knives, two whistles, a compass (there was no GPS available in that time period), four canteens, iodized purification tablets to kill the waterborne germs (bad water can kill, giardia is a consuming parasite that will consume the nutritional value of anything a person eats), one east wing hand ax, a machete long knife, a hunting knife, fishing gear, army jungle boots, an entrenching tool, head nets, four containers of mosquito repellent (the best repellents are Ben's 100 DEET and musk oil), a backpacker's cord, and a fanny pack full of first aid including sutures for sewing open wounds, antiseptic, six red air burst signals, and a signal mirror.

Failing to be fully prepared, or lacking proper education in the art of survival, can be disastrous. These factors contributed to the death of a young man several miles east of my homestead. He did not die from lack of food available. Rather, he could not overcome what was in his belly, eating the food before his body absorbed any nutritional value. He had contracted a tiny parasite, giardia, which multiplies as it is living in your small intestine. This causes a person to slowly perish from a diarrhea death. Commonly called beaver fever, the only cure is to take antibiotics as soon as possible.

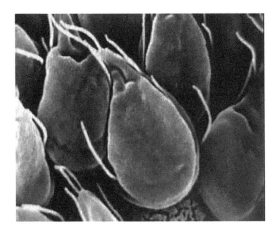

The parasite giardia

We were prepared to live off both the land and what we carried on our backs. While in the army, I was trained in the art of survival. Later on in my life, I became a scoutmaster for the young men of Wood Lake, Minnesota. I grew up having many experiences exploring the granite rock quarries in the rugged parts of the river valley of Minnesota. This was a place that I had nicknamed the Rocks.

A week prior to our trip, we holed up in Wasilla with Mickey Ose. We were busy making our final preparations, which included buying a short barrel Mossberg 12-gauge shotgun with a sling, 15 rounds of triple 000 buck, and 15 rounds of Magnum 3-inch slugs. This was our bear gun. Every other round loaded in the Mossberg short-barreled shotgun would be a slug, or 000 buck shot. We had brought enough freeze-dried backpacker's food to sustain us for a month. The .22 rifle would be used to hunt birds and rabbits, for a source of fresh meat. (Rabbit meat, however, is low on nutritional value.)

As a backup plan, I had bought more food than we could carry on our backs. We left the canned goods behind, inside the airstrip's building at Lake Minchumina. There is a storage building available for travelers flying out into the wild. We ended up leaving gear behind as well after I deemed it was too heavy; we could return for it later. We tied the excess gear high above the ground in order to keep it safe from bears. We left it hidden on the shoreline before we went inland to brave the godforsaken, uncharted territory. We blazed the tree to mark our cache.

Dan, turned fifteen near the end of June that year, and I was forty-three. Before leaving Wasilla heading to Fairbanks, Mickey had a long heart-to-heart talk with us. This was typical, given the caring person he is. He questioned my motive in making this trek into the wilderness. He wanted to be sure my reasoning was sound; most people cannot handle the total absence of civilization. Mickey is a people person, as many are. The difference is some are meant to live with people, and others prefer their own company. I am a social animal when it's necessary, but I'm also just as happy to be alone.

There are those who wanna be mountain men, big talkers who are unprepared for the reality of the wilderness. The dreamers that jump right into the great outdoors, without any experience or survival skills. Those are the ones that get themselves, and others, killed. Someday, there may be adventurers who want to follow in my footsteps because of my success in building a life of wilderness adventure. Let it be known that what I have accomplished was not achieved by chance. My success came from my skills, training, and experiences.

The future is what we make it. I had the foresight to realize I had a choice in forming my future, rather than leaving it to chance. Technology is improving at a fast rate in the field of communication for traveling. We only have to look to the past to see how fast new ideas advance. Technology is like dominoes, new products toppling the older versions before they can wear out. Progress will not stop anytime soon. I wanted to make sure I could stay ahead of it.

Cancer will be not only be cured, but preventable, in our near future. A day will come when science has advanced to the point of stopping, or controlling, the aging process. I may not live to see this, but some of you readers might.

The morning of July 2, we were on the road. It took us most of the day to drive the three hundred miles from Wasilla to Fairbanks. Our route of travel was on the Parks Highway.

Having eaten a late supper, we drove on the Parks Highway until we found a truck pullout. I parked the pickup, and we slept. The next morning after breakfast, we made our way to the International Airport of Fairbanks.

Tickets for a one-way flight to Lake Minchumina were $75 each per person, with a small charge for extra luggage. We were weighed along with our gear, and then our packs and gear were put in the storage compartments on the plane. I parked the pickup in the long-term storage lot, where it would be safe. The big day had finally arrived.

CHAPTER THREE: DAY 1

July 4, 1985

At the Fairbanks International Airport's main terminal, we went to the ticket counter to pay for our plane trip. The young lady working asked us if we were going to Lake Minchumina for trophy fishing. She continued to tell us that a lot of people go there for the big fish. I made the mistake of telling her that we were going on a hike to the federal land settlement area to find land to stake a claim. Her mouth said nothing, but her eyes screamed "crazy person." I resisted the urge to try and explain further because it was obvious her mind was made up. I said no more and walked away with my dignity (somewhat) intact.

The Chief Cherokee plane Dan and I flew on
to Lake Minchumina, July 4, 1985

This flying service was a small air taxi service, which had scheduled flights twice a week out to Lake Minchumina. This lake is the largest inland lake in Alaska. Lake Minchumina is only about twenty-five feet deep, but the fishing is great.

At one time, about forty-two people lived on the shores of Lake Minchumina. There was a time they even had a school. Currently (2014), there are less than nine people living there. The airfield located at Lake Minchumina has a weather cam–automated station, which anyone can pull up on the computer. It's a service used quite regularly by pilots. The airstrip itself was made for B-29 bombers during World War II. At that time, planes were ferried to Russia from this airfield.

While we were waiting for the plane to be loaded, Dan had a special request. He wanted a window seat. I said, "Sure, Dan."

The plane was parked on the tarmac; the time had come for us to board. Dan was looking all around.

"What are you looking for, Dan?"

"Is that small plane for us, Dad?"

"Sure is, Dan. I don't think you will have a problem finding a window seat. They're all window seats."

Our plane was a twin engine Chief Cherokee. This plane was capable of holding up to six passengers, two pilots, and cargo. The residents of the lake utilize this service for their supplies, flight service, and mail. At $75 one way, it was very reasonable to travel to town and back, unlike the disbursement of the private charter services.

At the lake's airstrip, there was a small shack that served as a post office. One of the female residents was the post office mistress. This post office is still operational to this day. However, only about nine people use it, twice a week. This post office has been on the chopping block list for some time but, somehow, has managed to survive—our tax dollars at work.

During the flight to Lake Minchumina, one of the passengers, a young lady with her child, struck up a conversation with us. She was going home after a shopping trip in Fairbanks. This woman had made several trips like this. As we traveled, she pointed out places of interest.

As we flew closer to Lake Minchumina, Bear Paw Mountains came into view. Shortly after, we could see Mount Roosevelt. We could also see the wide, meandering river below, named the Muddy River. The Muddy River is an outlet for the Lake Minchumina.

This was my first time seeing Lake Minchumina, other than on a map. It was very beautiful. There were many smaller lakes we could see from this bird's-eye view, as well as the lowlands surrounding the Muddy River. The higher hills to the northwest sported forests of white spruce and birch. From this vantage point, we could generally see the route that Dan and I would take. There were no roads or trails, only vast wilderness.

The few people that lived around the lake had a wonderful waterfront view. I can only imagine how rough that water could be in a windstorm. Boating on this lake could be treacherous, for sure; you would not want to be caught in a windstorm. Looking down at this lake, there were no boats to be seen. This is unlike the lakes in Minnesota; those lakes would be jam-packed with boats and water-skiers.

Other than seeing small cabins, dog yards, the airfield with runway lights, and a few buildings, it appeared as if we were in another world.

We started dropping altitude as we approached the airstrip. There was a crosswind on approach, forcing the pilot to tack into the wind, until it was the right time to straighten out. The wheels were lowered and locked. The plane straightened up just before the wheels touched the runway. It was a smooth touchdown, as we rolled to a stop.

It was only a few moments before the engines were turned off, and the post office lady was there for her mail exchange. A young man on a four-wheeler, which was hauling a trailer, drove up alongside the plane to haul cargo away. We all disembarked, and people began to approach us. The arrival of this airplane was akin to having a stagecoach arrive with the mail. They were also eager to see new people and returning neighbors.

I must describe the difference between going from living in the so-called civilized world and arriving in the middle of nowhere. In the civilized world, there is noise 24-7. Out here, after all engines were turned off, there were only people's voices. When those voices are quiet, there is a deafening silence. I have adapted to being in absolute silence in the wilderness; for me it is a feeling of comfort. For the average city person, the absence of sound can cause a lonely, insecure feeling. The oppressing silence can feel depressing and cause anxiety.

The pilot announced it was time to go. He had a reason for being hasty to leave. The mosquitoes, jillions of them, were approaching. You could hear the swarm preparing to attack us, the *zzzzz* noise was getting louder, as they closed in on us.

In Fairbanks, they have mosquito control. Out here, it was every man, woman, and beast for themselves. Fortunately, I anticipated this from my prior experience and had a bottle of mosquito repellent in my pocket. Daniel said, "Gee-whiz, thanks, Dad."

"Wait until we have to use the head nets on a cloudy day. That's when they are really bad."

Today was the Fourth of July. The locals had prepared to set off fireworks at midnight, the darkest time of the day. This time of year, the hours of daylight were still long, twenty-one hours with the sun up. June 22, or thereabout, is the longest day of full sun. It can last all twenty-four hours at certain latitudes. Even during the hours the sun is down, it is still light enough out to read.

Along with the fireworks, there was a rock skipping contest. This was a yearly event, held on a spit of land that extended out from the shoreline. The contestants used the flat lake stones found on the beach.

We were quickly greeted and invited to celebrate the Fourth of July. This was a tempting offer; it would have been a great opportunity to meet everybody, but I had other plans.

A couple of men and a woman approached us, inquiring about what we were going to do. This was not like being in a big town, where we would have gone largely ignored. Here, we were strangers for only a short time. Upon learning that we were headed out on a monthlong journey into the wilderness, the woman gasped and looked at Dan.

The locals continued to tell us that seven other groups had tried to do what we were planning. They informed us that none made it and most came back within a day. One voyager was gone for over a week. He went in unprepared, and without mosquito repellent. He thought he could live off the land with only a pocketknife.

When this traveler made it back to the airstrip, he said that he had contemplated killing himself. The circumstance that had driven him to consider suicide was the mosquitoes, black flies, and all the other bloodsucking bugs. He was being drained of blood, getting eaten alive. He had lost significant weight and had not eaten. His flesh was like that of raw meat—swollen red, a bad rash, overall looking infected. His appearance was like that of a burn victim, or so we were told.

This news only encouraged me to push on even more. I was confident that my experiences would lead me to be successful.

After the woman left, a native man spoke with us. He casually eyed our supplies as we visited, as if he was wondering whether we had what it took to make such an adventure. He advised us that it was not the bears we should worry about but the Little People. I did not ask what he meant by that. I was thinking he was only trying to express his beliefs, or something along those lines. He struck me as being serious though, and he said this to us in confidence while looking over his shoulder.

It was not until June of 1987 that I had an up close experience with the Little People. This is also a story I am saving for another book.

With that conversation over, we went about checking our gear. We planned on leaving our surplus supplies, the extra food, and some extra clothing in a locked storage building. They would be kept safe, in the event we returned for whatever reason. My plan was much the same as the sixty-four homesteaders already out there. There would be a plane we could catch a ride to town on after our trip, whether I found land to claim or not.

Mind you, staking was something that had to be well thought out. I wanted to be sure of my choice by setting my boots on the ground. I never buy anything without first inspecting it. Like a partner, compatibility and love are the key deciding factors. The land itself would call to me.

"Are we ready, Dan?" My mountain pack, with all the attached gear on my belt, weighed close to a hundred pounds. Dan's external frame pack, with the attached gear, was close to eighty pounds. We would be running in super low gear, moving with this amount of weight. In the case of the slow and steady turtle, he won the race, same as it would be with us.

The previous year, I used topographic maps to plan the general route we would take, to be adjusted as needed.

"Where's the yellow brick road, Dad?"

"The shoreline, headed that way."

Having a late start, we did not make it far this day. It was the beginning of establishing our routine. This airstrip is on the southwest shore, and we had to travel westward before we could go inland to the high ground. Once on high ground, we would go northwest, following along the shore, with a bit of travel in the woods. This would be our easiest part of the hike.

Lake Minchumina shoreline and the last wooden barge
to make it up the river from Nenana left to rot

CHAPTER FOUR: DAY 2

July 5, 1985

Dan at our campsite on the shore of Lake Minchumina. You
can see the Alaskan mountain range in the background.

Morning came sunny and bright, with a light breeze off the
lake. This breeze, combined with being on the shore, kept
the mosquitoes away. Our tent was a four-man Eureka
with a rain fly and was a breathable tent. We made pancakes for
breakfast, using our silver tone frying pan and a portable folding
grill. This grill was attached to the outside of my pack.

Laugh if you must, but this hike was not your ordinary hike. It
was a one-way hike off of the beaten path. In fact, there was no path

at all. We would be traveling (most likely) where no human had gone before, once we left the lake.

This morning's view was an inspiration. We were camped on the shore of the largest inland lake and about six miles from the geographical center of Alaska. We had a clear view of Denali Mountain and its range. Denali Mountain is the highest mountain in North America, coming in at 20,320 feet in elevation.

As we traveled along, the shore began to narrow and became rocky. We came to a point where it was no longer possible to follow the shore. Looking further ahead, it was clear to me that we would have to leave the shoreline. Where we had stopped, the water was too deep to wade in any longer. We had no choice but to climb a high hill, going over the top, then back down to the shoreline.

As we were climbing this hill, a plane landed and came to shore where we had been the day before. Two people disembarked. First was the pilot, who was the owner and operator of a flying guiding service for the paying tourist. The other was a tourist. I could only imagine the expense this cost the tourist. They went into the woods and headed to the high ground. They wanted a lookout view of the lake and the mountains some sixty miles distant.

We stayed motionless until they left to give this tourist his time to feel alone, getting his money's worth. They never noticed us some eighty feet away, in the thick forest of white and black spruce. After they left, we were ready to move on. We needed the rest. It was a welcome break, rather than a disturbance.

We crossed the top of the hill and continued on. A short distance inland, we come across a well-used trail. It was favorable to the direction we were headed. It leads us to a sizable cabin, lived in by a man and woman. The man was busy tending to his dogs. We introduced ourselves to the woman to ease her mind. They were residents of the community. Most likely, they had already heard of us.

The lady went on to tell us the best she could about what we were in for on this journey. Looking at Daniel, she straight on asked him what he thought about the information she had just shared with us. Dan responded without hesitation, "Thanks for your concern, lady, but we will be fine. This hike has been planned and prepared for, for over a year. My dad has spent most of his life gaining the experience that prepared him for this task, ma'am."

She added that we would be on our own, in case of an emergency. "It will be buggy, and the walking will be treacherous." She said this as she was looking at our heavy packs, shotgun, a .22 rifle, and the metal detector in our hands.

I noticed that look. "Whatever we might need is in these packs. You should realize that we have planned for a long, arduous hike. We were told of the seven parties that turned back. They were unprepared, and it was wise of them to turn back. We might have to as well. In fact, we left extra food in the shack by the post office. We are prepared for such a scenario."

As a former scoutmaster, I was well versed in "be prepared," the Scout's motto. I was not some fool that was about to try to survive on only a pocketknife. We had spent a year preparing. I addressed the lady's concern regarding medical emergencies, by pointing to my fanny pack. This pack has all the medical supplies needed. I assure you, I have prepared well.

We continued on our trip, leaving the couple behind. We were following what must have been a winter trail. We made our way from the winter trail, to the shoreline, working our way through the steep terrain. In short order, we were presented with an obstacle—our first encounter with the matted jungle mossy floor. There was brush, snags, branches to stoop under, and we often had to climb over the continuous debris. It was an arduous crawling pace of travel. This is was what was in store for us for the next month. In some areas, the moss covering the ground was all of two feet thick. The moss had many surprises for us, hidden from view.

Eventually, we made our way back to the shore. There were times while traveling along the shore that we had to wade through water. It was a true test for our jungle combat boots. They would get wet, but then the water would drain. So far they passed the test. When we were finally done wading in the water, our pant legs were wet. The winds off the lake had a cooling effect on our wet clothing. As a precaution, we changed our jeans. We hung our wet jeans on our packs to dry as we walked.

Dan resting in place with his full gear still on

The heavy packs forced us to move at a slow pace. We were also hampered by needing to rest every chance we had. Luckily, there were convenient bench rests, which nature contributed. Finding a place to rest without having to unload our packs allowed us to have five-minute breaks. This way we could quickly continue with our progress. Sitting on the ground with a heavy pack wasn't a problem while resting, but it was no fun in getting back up. To remove the packs and then put them back on was a two-person job—difficult for either of us to do on our own.

Dan was the first to spot a deadfall, which was pulled from the ground roots and all. Dan sat on it, giving a sigh of relief, enjoying a break from hauling his extra eighty pounds. Dan was smiling from ear to ear as I just stood there resting in place.

Suddenly, his smile left. We heard a little crack, then another. Dan just looked at me with surprise as the tree dropped the rest of the way to the ground with a loud crunch! Thousands of ants were madly milling about. It was a funny sight. I had to capture this on the camera before I helped him get up from the ground. The full pack held him down, like a turtle lying on its back.

We continued to travel a little farther before we picked out a high sandbar to stop for the night. We set up the tent, started a cooking fire, and ate some of our food that was weighing us down. After supper, there was still plenty of light out, so we just relaxed and took in the sights while sitting at the campfire. Looking into the woods away from the shore, we saw a jungle. We couldn't help but wonder how our inland trip was going to play out, guessing at the difficulties we would face.

I told Dan, "The woods are the thickest near the bottom of a hill, thinning out as the ground rises in elevation. The bottoms have more moisture, making for dense willows, alder, and a tangle of brush. We are going to stay up on the top, only going down when we have to. We may have to descend to the bottom lands in order to reach another hill. We will head back up to the ridgetops as quickly as possible. The route will not be direct but will allow for easier traveling. This will save us time, give us less risk of falling, and minimize our travel through all that overgrown jungle. My previous hiking experiences in Alaska have taught me that lesson. There is good news. Here, north of the range, we are lucky there is no devil's club. That is a nasty shrub with large leaves, which hide two-inch-long sharp thorns on the underside of the leaves—leaves that are as big as elephant ears and can rip your clothes and flesh to shreds."

Devil's club can be found when hiking in the Matanuska Valley, by Sutton and Palmer. South of the Alaskan Mountain Range, that plant is at the base of all the hills as well as on the bushy lowlands.

"That Mossberg 12-gauge shotgun, Dan, has six rounds. They range from triple 000 buck to a single slug, and all are magnums. Well then, let's see what they can do? See those tall tree stumps over there? The taller one that's ten inches in diameter, Dan! Stand back fifteen feet, aim, and fire at the midsection. Pretend that it's a bear."

Dan was all for this. "Yeah!" It was our first time trying this new weapon. *Kerr boom*! No more tree.

"Holy cow!" Dan said. "I blew it away."

"Now you know what a triple 000 buck does. Try the next round. It's a three-inch single slug magnum. Go for the tree next to the one you just shot."

Dan took aim and fired! *Kerr boom*!

"Wow-we wow, holy cow!" Dan said. The single slug made a one-inch hole on this side of the tree and busted up the tree into splinters going out the backside.

The pump-action shotgun was loaded full of six rounds. For safety reasons, we never had a round in the chamber, except when it was necessary. My policy was never to have a round in the chamber until needed. The shotgun was loaded with interchanging rounds, using single slugs and triple 000 bucks.

After supper, we called it a day. Before we were fully settled in, we heard the sound of a motorboat. This brought us out of the tent. It was some of the people we had met at the airstrip.

They visited with us for a bit and offered to come back in the morning. They wanted to give us ride to a shoreline where we could move inland. Their offer would save us two days, at least. It was agreed upon. They headed off after we all exchanged, "See you in the morning."

CHAPTER FIVE: DAY 3

July 6, 1985

Along the breezy shore, we could keep relatively mosquito free. We were enjoying breakfast and the coolness of the morning. "It's time to break camp, Dan." We got everything ready and waited for our boat ride. We heard someone calling us from the lake.

"Ahoy ashore!"

"Good morning!" Our new friend had a twenty-foot flat-bottomed boat. We put our gear in first and then climbed in. He asked us where we wanted to be dropped off. I pointed to the spot and off we went.

This gentleman was in the process of building a new cabin down the shore a ways. It sat about three hundred feet back from the shore, in the woods. On this day, he was just beginning to set the piling concrete posts for the foundation, which would support the cabin. In this area, there is permafrost, and that was the only correct way of building a structure on permafrost ground. The ground under the cabin must remain cool and covered with moss. If it's not, a cabin will sink, as so many others have. As the permafrost thaws slowly, inch by inch, any structure on top of it will sag down with it.

We asked our new friend how much it cost for him to live here. He replied, "About $100 per month. When I need money, I hop a flight to Fairbanks. I go to the job hall for a cash job or a longer surveying job." He was a surveyor by trade.

It only took about five minutes and we reached the shore. "Thank you very much, sir." He wished us luck and turned about, heading back out on the lake. This ride saved us a lot of time, energy, supplies, and hard effort. My guess is that boat ride saved us two days' worth of travel. There was a boggy inlet we would have had to bypass by traveling upstream until we could cross over, before heading up the hill. That was one segment of our journey I was glad to have a shortcut around.

We found a spot on this shoreline to hang the gear we would be leaving behind. We sorted through our supplies to see which items we could spare. We were lightening our load but making sure we carried everything essential for a successful mission.

I thought of the early homesteaders making their cross-country journeys. They, too, had to lighten their loads on the way as well. The glass they carried with them was the foremost savored item. They cherished their windows. However, they would bring even crazier things, like a piano.

What we decided to leave behind was the extra changes of clothes, the rest of our canned goods, fishing rods (keeping only the line and hooks), rain pants, and a few other nonessential items, like that a weekend camper on wheels might bring.

In the days of our ancestors, proper hygiene was lax. Some people would bathe and do their laundry only once or twice a year. We were going to have to pick up some of the habits of those days. There would be no way to wash our clothing until our trip was over.

All the items we were leaving behind filled an army duffel bag. "There, Dan. Our packs are lighter now." I tossed one end of our rope over a limb way up high and hoisted the bag up. I made sure it was out of sight, for neither man nor bear to see. I blazed a nearby tree, like the pirates of old marking their treasure. We used fifty feet of our one hundred feet rope, keeping our gear safe up high.

We still had fifteen days' worth of backpackers' dehydrated food, Salisbury steaks, and several other choice meals. All were lightweight, sealed, and safe.

Our last view of Lake Minchumina before
heading into the Alaskan jungle

From here on, we would have to be very careful and analyze each step we took. We could not afford an injury. We would be on our own, far from the lake and the civilization that lived there.

To make our way up the next forested long sloping hill would take the better part of a day. I left Dan behind with the gear while I went ahead with red surveyor's tape, using it to mark a trail. The hill had a gradual slope for a good half mile, rounding to a level plain as it reached the top. Once I made it to this point, travel became easier. Several hours had passed, as I worked my way to the hilltop. Once I reached the hill's summit, I turned back and headed down to the shore where Dan was waiting.

There was no trail to the shore; our path was full of alder trees and a tangle of weeping alder limbs. I studied the rugged terrain and laid out the course we would take. Going back down the hill, using my long machete knife, I cleared away the limbs. After the arduous work of climbing, flagging, and hacking away the brush, it was not hard to decide to stop for the night and make camp. We would have a long day of work come morning.

Our goal was to make the journey safely. In order to do this, we needed to follow our own rules carefully. This meant going slowly, thinking every choice through three times, before making a decision.

As we traveled, I was frequently checking my compass. I made no shortcuts. We would travel through birch forest whenever possible because a spruce forest is obstructing. We followed the high ground as much as we could. Following these rules made traveling safer.

There was less moss-covered ground, less brush, and we could see far ahead. This helped us to maintain our bearings by using landmarks. We could get a general idea of our position on the maps by eyeballing landmarks, helping us decide which way to go. The low areas would be a jungle and impede our travel. This was a North American wilderness jungle—not suitable for a horse and rider.

I've observed the terrain of Lake Minchumina from a bird's-eye view. The rock in the lake had been turned into smooth gravel. The stones had been rounded and worn down from the action of the water. The stone that was outside of the lake showed no signs of wear; that stone was rectangular and jagged. The rock in this area is cubical black basalt rock.

There was some shale gravel, but most of the rock in this area is cubical basalt, with a mix of quartz. What I had observed during the two days of traveling on the lake, was while the lake had worn stones, the rest of the rock was not disturbed and had not moved since it was formed.

There was not much soil covering the bedrock, except in the pockets and boggy ground. No volcanic ash or silt. The ice sheet covering this part of the earth had not moved and scoured the rock surfaces. The ice had melted in the place it was formed, creating lakes, tundra ponds, and meandering rivers. There are still a few places covered by the remaining glacial ice. Over time, the ice has been covered with windblown dust. This makes a soil-covered hill with a solid ice core. The remaining ice sheets are shielded from the sun and warming air.

It is not uncommon to dig into the permafrost soil covering an ice core and collect ice formed millions of years ago. Millions of years of extreme, penetrating cold has left the ground frozen down deep. The ground is frozen a thousand feet deep in some regions of Alaska.

I have seen windblown, drifted sand dunes on the Tanana River flats, similar to snow drifts in the Midwestern states after a blizzard.

Snowdrifts formed from the wind blowing in one direction. On the flight out from Fairbanks, I saw not only windblown sand dunes, but puddling. Within twenty- to thirty-mile proximity of here, the puddling was generally absent. Most of the ground had a covering of moss and trees, disguising the pocked landscape.

There are small tundra ponds, some of which were in the center of a circle of ridged outcrops. They looked as though the ground under the ponds had collapsed. The centers sunk, which formed ridges around the edges, much like the rings left standing in the mud when a stone is dropped into it. I refer to these as puddling. Something is under those puddling areas; I suspect oil, gas, or both.

Also, to see exposed rock from the air is rare. The only exposed rock visible is in places where there is erosion of the sod, such as on the steep river banks and shorelines. The rocks in the Alaskan terrain has been covered by windblown materials, like the sand in the desert of Arabia—save for here, in the central area of Alaska. In Central Alaska, there is green vegetation covering the wind-drifted debris. But what do I know? I have no degree. I am only a simple rock hound here on planet earth. Are you getting the idea now as to why I carry a metal detector and the dowsing rods?

CHAPTER SIX: DAY 4

July 7, 1985

After having a big breakfast, we loaded up and took one last look at the lake before starting our ascent into the interior land. The real test of our journey was now at hand. It was like climbing out of the trenches onto a battlefield, going forward into the unknown of God's land.

We stopped to put on our head nets, covering over our hats, and tucked tightly down into our shirt. We put on leather gloves, after applying Ben's 100 DEET. This is the best mosquito repellent, in my opinion. It's used only on clothing though, not on the skin. We made sure these precautions were taken against the swarms that would be assaulting us once we set foot in the forest of darkness. Black flies, horse flies, mosquitoes, no-see-ums, and every bloodsucking bug known to man were awaiting our attendance, except wood ticks. Lucky for us.

If we left any of our skin exposed, it would be ripe for the taking. We wanted to avoid becoming a meal for millions of insects. Thus, even our hands had to be covered with gloves. It wasn't the cold temperatures that forced us to be fully covered. July is the hottest time of the year in Alaska, reaching one hundred degrees during midday. The temperatures in the interior of Alaska are colder in the winter and hotter in the summer than they are in the coastal areas, such as Anchorage.

After two hours of hiking, we reached the summit. This was a long time to cover the short length of ground we traversed, but considering what we had to go through, it really was not bad. Our Vietnam jungle combat boots were already proving themselves. The sole inserts kept our feet from getting blisters.

Checking with a topographic map, we were planning a route that would take us in a northeastern direction. The ground was fairly flat, with no drainage. Black spruce was the most prevalent tree. There was a moss covering the ground that was two feet thick and very treacherous.

The dense and dark black spruce forest we were heading into

We were unable to see much more than twenty-five to fifty feet ahead. This didn't present much of a problem as we had a compass to rely on. It was a very dark, closed-in forest. I couldn't help but think of open spaces because of the lack of it here. A feeling of claustrophobia started pressing in on me.

Claustrophobia was an unwelcome guest, showing up frequently throughout our trip. It was unnerving to travel by the compass's lead, not knowing what lay ahead. I did my best to ensure we followed the highest terrain to avoid ever going into a ravine. Only being able to see landmarks infrequently meant we could be meandering. I found myself referring to the compass more and more often. We constantly had to stop for water breaks. I was well aware of the dangers of dehydration. It is of utmost importance to hydrate often.

Having a large two-quart canteen and two smaller one-quart canteens was crucial for us to have a successful trip. We were always on the lookout for water sources. The sights and sounds of flowing water were always a pleasure to hear. I stated earlier the importance of pure drinking water. We didn't purify water by boiling it on this trip. Rather, we used iodized tablets to purify any water we found. One pill per quart, shaken not stirred.

Only rainwater, or water coming from a flowing source, was deemed safe to drink. Topographic maps are very useful in locating water. You can identify a water source on the map, which is represented by lines that are drawn showing the likely waterways. The suspected water sources were always our target when deciding where to make camp.

A few times we traveled through the night, not making camp until the next morning. We needed to be sure we made camp near a water source in order to replenish our canteens. We needed water for washing and cooking at each camp, as well as refilling our drinking supply.

When there was stone available, we could build a safer fire. Heating the coals on the stone meant less danger of sparking a forest fire. We needed water in order to ensure any fires we lit were completely extinguished when it was time to go. It would be easy to start a forest fire. A hot coal could smolder for days before reigniting. I would not have enjoyed looking back to see a fire raging behind us. This is and was a very real danger due to rotted vegetation on the forest floor.

I cannot emphasize enough the danger of failing to fully extinguish a fire in the wild of Alaska. The rotting roots covering most of the ground are like a slow burning fuse, eventually reaching tinder debris, and exploding into fire. Wherever there was stone available, we made a small rock-walled campfire. We termed these firepit altars.

Instead of tearing down the altars, we left them standing. Someone might come across them in the future and find them useful.

If we had to come back this way, the campsites would be our guide and save us from the work of rebuilding a firepit. At each of our campsites, we would deeply blaze a tree and flag the area with our survey tape. That way our signatures could easily be seen from a distance.

Dan cooking on one of the altars we built

While we were traveling, we would mark a healthy tree every so often. We would blaze the trees on both sides so they could readily be seen from either direction. In order to properly blaze a tree, you need to expose the heartwood, not just mark in the bark. We had to take precautionary measures, should a search party need to come find us, or our remains.

In the dark areas of the forest, under the moss, there was ice. We would use this ice for cooking our freeze-dried packages of food. Since our food was sealed, we could use unfiltered water. We needed to save our precious purified water for drinking.

Try as we might to stay high up on top of the ridges, there were still times we had to go down. It was the only way to reach a new ridge while still staying on course.

This was one of those days in which we had to fight our way through the lowland undergrowth. I felt less than human traveling in the dark, dense, black spruce forest. Seeing only six feet in any direction and relying only on a compass needle gave me a heavy, foreboding feeling, an invisible weight pressing from all sides. The end of the eighteen-hour day came, and we had not reached a creek. Nor could we see landmarks to help us locate where we were on the map. We knew we were headed in the right direction; we had the compass. The question was, where are we?

Drinking lots of water was important but not to the point that we would run out. There were times we had to ration to be safe. That was the case on this day.

We cleared an area for the tent and a firepit. There was no rock. However, beneath the moss cover was plenty of ice and hard frozen ground. The folding grill with legs worked well. We added more dry moss where the tent was going to be set up. This made for comfortable sleep. The tent had a cloth floor but was not waterproof. To avoid getting our things wet, we used a clear poly sheet, which was cut to size before the start of our trip. After the tent was set up, we placed our sleeping bags and packs inside, leaving only the cooking tools outside.

Never leave a tent unattended—bear, moose, or other animals, can and will destroy it and its contents. It has been my experience that you need a tent sized for four men, at the minimum, in order to house two serious backpackers and their gear. The Eureka tent is lightweight, durable, breathable, and bug tight.

The army has two-man pup tents that are so small, even a squirrel gets caught up in them trying to escape in a hurry. There was a time in my life when I was an army aggressor. When we would do war game exercises, I would play the role of an attacking enemy (i.e., army aggressor). The soldiers in pup tents would get caught up and had no way to get out or fight back. I tagged many a soldier while they were struggling to get free of their pup tents during our war training.

Still needing to conserve our water for drinking, I used my pocketknife and a hand ax to remove the thick layer of moss and collected the icy frozen earth. I placed a layer of this frozen moist matter in the pan, followed by the sealed foil package of steak. I added a covering of ice and cooked it until it was done. (One does what they must in order to survive in the Alaskan wilderness).

Supper was delicious. It tamed the lion that had been growling in my stomach. "Do you want me to heat some water up for doing dishes, Dad?"

"Nope, tonight we will use moss to scrub our cookware clean. The moss works as a disinfectant at the same time. We need to conserve the water, and melting ice would take too much time and resources. The ice would have to come to a rolling boil for twenty minutes, before it would be germ free. Moss works better."

Once we headed into the tent for the night, we could finally remove our head nets and gloves. "Dan, before you remove anymore, I need you to do one more thing."

"What's that, Dad?"

"Close the zipper, Dan. How many mosquitoes made it in here already?"

"Eight or ten, Dad."

"Dan, use a half inch length of Pic off of a full coil of Pic. Because we're closed in a small area, using the whole coil might kill us. A half inch will do. Watch and learn, Dan."

I held a lit match to the piece of Pic coil. It began to glow and smoke. The mosquitoes were buzzing about. As they were flitting around, they would fly over the smoke rising from the Pic. When they flew into the smoke, they dropped dead instantly with a thud. Crazy as it sounds, we could hear their bodies hitting the floor.

"Neat, Dad! Let me finish off the rest." From then on, Dan took care of the mosquitoes in the tent.

As we settled in for the night, we talked of the following day's hike, guessing how many miles we might get. At some point, we fell fast asleep. I am a light sleeper, and any noise other than the natural sounds of us sleeping would wake me. Thankfully, this night was uneventful. We were in very high spirits and tired. We needed a good sleep.

CHAPTER SEVEN: DAY 5

July 8, 1985

We awoke to a rainy, drizzly day. It was a welcome cool and cloudy forecast. The Vikings knew the weather, and from their culture came the saying, "Red sky in the morning, sailors take warning, red sky at night, sailor's delight." I, too, am a Viking, and I trust this ancient knowledge to be true.

This drizzly day would not be a good one for traveling. Besides, Dan was coming down with a cold. I made a shelter to keep our cooking fire dry and then made pancakes for breakfast.

I decided to hunker down until the next day, leaving our camp set up. "Dan, you stay warm and dry and get rested up for tomorrow. Try to fight off that cold." We had cold medicine and aspirin to fight the oncoming cold. I stayed outside; my plan was to work on a trail to follow the next day, flagging it.

This rainy day presented a wonderful opportunity to replenish our water supply. I made sure this was done before I set off to flag the trail. In front of the tent, I made a lean-to out of poles to support the poly sheeting. I had Dan's help in doing this.

We placed our poly sheeting over the lean-to, making a sloping surface area of 15' × 8'. This worked pretty well; the water ran down into a basin we formed out of the end of the piece of poly sheeting.

It was cold and wet, but thankfully the high end of the lean-to had proven to be a good shelter over our small campfire. The dry wood we had stacked under the lean-to earlier gave us a convenient supply of dry firewood. After all this work in setting up a dry camp, once the water catch system was completed, I sent Dan back into the tent to keep warm for the rest of the day.

I started working on the trail ahead, hacking out the brush and marking it. I was marking this trail for Dan to help him locate me should I not return in a timely manner. I worked the rest of the day on blazing the trail ahead. I tried to make good time by going the way of least resistance.

The black spruce forest was dark, thick, and buggy. When it was raining hard, the bugs went under the shelter of the leaves. Each step on the moss floor, and each bumping of a leafy bush, sent the mosquitoes swarming. They all wanted to get a taste of me. Not all of the repellent on my clothing had washed off in the rain, but they were attracted to my body heat. There were times when I would turn to get an alignment of my trail, and there would be a black cloud of them sizing me up for dinner. Without covered skin or repellent, I could easily see how a person could go mad. Mosquitoes do not sleep. They're active 24-7. However, on a bright sunny day, they do head for the shade. Sunshine, wind, and bug repellent have become some of my best friends.

After supper, Dan was feeling better. The warm food, bed rest, medicine, and keeping warm must have helped. Obviously, the strenuous workout had taken its toll on both of us. We needed to adjust our speed to slow and easy, or else we would soon burn out. We had many days and a lot of miles yet to travel. We had to remain vigilant to adapt to all situations as they arose.

CHAPTER EIGHT: DAY 6

July 9, 1985

Morning sunlight was streaming through the forest top. Fog hovered over us, and dew covered all the foliage. We woke to a symphony performance by the local bird population. This would be a new and wonderful day. We had done the right thing by holing up for a day. The rain had stopped. It was like we were being watched over by our guardian angels.

We hung our rain gear high up in a tree on the shoreline to dry before packing it up. Dan made pancakes for breakfast. When we were done eating, we took down the tent. The tent had become heavier due to the rain. We couldn't waste valuable time waiting for it to dry.

Checking on the water that had collected, I asked Dan, "What do you think? Filling the canteens shouldn't be a problem."

"Boy, I'll say! There must be thirty gallons of water there, and all pure drinking water too. Dad, I'm sure glad we brought the eleven pounds of poly. It has paid for itself just using it this one time."

One by one, Dan filled up the canteens with his canteen cup. We drank a lot of water, feeling like a camel readying for a trip through the desert.

"What do we do with the rest of the water, Dad?"

"We will use the fire pit to store the water in, once it has cooled down. Using poly sheeting, we will enclose the water, making an improvised container. We can then cover it with heavy timber and moss, keeping it out of sight."

"It's unlikely we will return for this water, but it's prudent to keep the extra stashed away as a precaution. We scouts must be prepared in every way possible. I'm going to call this campsite Rainy Day Camp."

"Well, Dan! Are you ready to move out? We should be up on a hill by the end of the day. From that vantage point, we should be able to see landmarks. By locating three landmarks on the map, we should be able to pinpoint our position."

We set off for the day to continue our hike. As we traveled along, I noticed a few details of our surrounding habitat that Dan might find interesting.

"This is moose country, for sure. It's full of willows, and the ground is covered with moose nuggets, just like a barnyard. Up on this hill, there is a breeze giving the moose some relief from mosquitoes. It also looks like it might be good for grazing." There were also many indicators that this area attracted all kinds of animals, along with the moose.

Later in the day, we came upon a black spruce forest. Within this forest, we found a pine squirrel and his pine cone cache. This squirrel had built himself a castle. His feeding/collecting/storage area measured ten feet in diameter and was four feet high.

The squirrels that built this huge home must
have been around for many generations

The squirrels harvest pine cones from the surrounding trees in clusters while they are still green. The new cones are added to the century-old pile of empty husks. They spend the year collecting new cones, leaving them untouched, until the winter months. During the winter, they peel and eat the seeds, discarding the husk on the ever-growing pile. Hidden by these piles of pine cone husks are escape routes and burrows.

This particular squirrel pile was built up among several smaller trees. This made it hard for the bear to dig after the squirrel. "Look up into the tree, Dan. See that nice comfy nest? That's a squirrel's home. This spot is his comfort zone. He has escape routes and trees to climb. A big pile of pine cones for daily meals. This squirrel can rest in peace here. He has much less fear of being caught here than he would be in other places. There are many generations in his family. See how the pile has been knocked down and spread about? More than a few times a bear has tried to dig after that squirrel. This is one old, determined squirrel."

Reading the compass, which was difficult
with the camouflaged head net

We left the squirrel haven and continued our hike. Sometime later that day, Dan asked me to hurry up. "You're always checking that compass, sometimes every fifty feet."

"You're right, Dan. This is new country for me. It would not be hard to get turned around. I can't see any landmarks to help me stay on track. Most of the time, we are in heavy cover, and we can't see very far ahead. That will change as we work our way further inland. Since we are on that topic, Dan, we need to get a view of some landmarks to get our bearings. I sure would like to know where we are. Climb that spruce tree, Dan."

Dan climbing high up to get a better look at our surroundings

"When you get up there, tell me what landmarks you see. When you climb back down, point out the hills you see on this map. Then I will be able to locate our position on the map. It has been two days since we last knew our exact location. We could be anywhere. We've been heading in the general direction all this time."

"Okay, Dad. Up I go."

The tree was a big black spruce with a shallow root system. He needed to be extra careful. At least he had the mosses covering the ground to break his fall, should he come crashing down.

I could see the ground covering the roots moving. "Be careful, Dan. That tree does not have much of a root system. It only has the moss securing the roots. A good wind could bring it down." Carefully, Dan made his way up. The tree swayed slightly, as Dan ascended.

Dan was close to the top of the spindly tree and could go no higher. I shouted out, "What do you see?"

He answered back, "Taller trees." The forest was too flat, only other trees could be seen. Dan made his way back down.

"Sorry, Dad, I couldn't see anything but taller trees."

"That's okay. At least you tried. The tree is still standing, and you're safely down. For now, we have no choice but to depend on the compass. At least we have that much to keep us from wandering in circles. This time of the year, it's hard to know the direction by looking at the sun. At some point, we will be able to figure where we are." We continued to push on.

Nearly eighteen hours of traveling passed before we reached the high ground. We could once again view the world. "This is good, Dan. I feel free!" Being enclosed in the forest, unable to see any distance ahead, is not for me. Give me a valley. I want miles and miles of clear views and open air.

From our new standpoint, we were able to see the earth's horizon in the hazy distance. We were finally able to triangulate our position on the topographic map using landmarks and my compass. Two of the landmarks we used were Haystack Mountain, and Bear Paw Mountain. I could rest easy knowing we were still on track. (I did not have a GPS instrument in the year of 1985.)

"We are at this point, Dan." I pointed out our location on the map. "See that long flat hill? Off in the distance?" There were several valleys between where we stood and our final destination.

"That's a long ways, Dad. How far?" Laying out the big map, I measured the distance while showing Dan how this was done. "Thirty miles, Dan. By air. That doesn't include all the miles walking up and down hills, zigzagging around obstacles. Our walking miles will add up to much more than thirty."

As we walked, we entered a clearing. There was a long meadow with few trees. It was eerily out of place. This was not a normal piece of land, at least not compared to the forest we had thus far encountered. The moss was thin. I could feel the bedrock under my feet as I walked.

Dan was ahead of me, looking at the ground. "Come quick, Dad! What do you make of this?"

I caught up with Dan and looked down at partially exposed white stone. "That's quartz, Dan!" With our boots and army entrenching spade, we scraped away debris, exposing more of the stone. We uncovered a wide vein of quartz, mixed with gray and black rock. "Hand me the metal detector."

I adjusted the settings and turned it on. Holding the metal detector, I kept the pad hovering just above the ground. I started moving it side to side, like you would do when sweeping a floor. Immediately, the detector went *zzzz-zzz-zz*. The loud noise reverberated through the forest. The needle was pegging off the meter.

"Holy cow," Dan said, "let me try that!" He swept the detector above the ground, getting the same results I did.

"Alright, Dan. I'm going to map out this rock and try to get a close estimate of its size." It was about four feet wide and ran over a hundred yards in length before continuing on into the thin black spruce cover. I could not see any greenish tint in the quartz itself, but the quartz was mixed with a large amount of a lead gray material.

Using the entrenching spade and hand ax, we pried out a bread pan–sized chunk of the gray rock. I broke off a corner off the gray rock. The exposed rock was a lighter color of gray. The air exposed surfaces were closer to a black color. With two hands, I handed the big hunk to Dan to hold. Dan nearly dropped it. "That's heavy! It is a lot heavier than a normal rock of that size, Dad!"

"Yeah, it's about a hundred pounds, Dan. Put it in your pack so you can haul it out with us?"

"You're funny, Dad. No way. Maybe a piece of it, okay?"

We marked this spot on the map and piled up rocks to make a four-foot-high marker. I placed a claim on this mineral location by putting our names and the date in a tin foil bag and placed this in the center of our marker.

A claim on a mineral location doesn't mean that you own the land, but that you own the rights to the minerals. A landowner doesn't own the rights to minerals on their property exclusively, unless they claim it. Anyone has the right to come and work it if they file for rights first and have it recorded in the land office for that area. Of course the claim must be worked; a person cannot just sit on it, to hold indefinitely.

I went on explaining to Dan, "This is a hard rock, like silver ore. It could also be what is known as galena. Galena is a mixture of all sorts of minerals and lead. That is why it was so heavy in comparison to its size." Someday, I will return to this remotely located spot.

We decided to set up camp for the night. Even though it was late in the day, the sun was brightly shining. This was a fine place to rest—high up on solid rock, with a thin carpet of moss, and a view overlooking the vast wilderness. We had plenty of water in our canteens, it was close to paradise.

While I built a rock-enclosed altar for our campfire, Dan was going to scrounge around with the .22 rifle. "I have the urge for fresh meat, Dad." Leaving his pack at camp, he headed off.

"Bring your signal whistle, and keep an eye on where you are at all times. This is new country, you could easily become lost."

I was fully enjoying this chance to rest unencumbered from my carrying pack. Ahh! It was so relaxing. I was busy gathering firewood when I heard a shot. Good. One shot usually means a kill. A few moments later, I heard another shot, followed by a third. Three shots close together would be a distress signal, but these shots were sporadic. After hearing all the shooting, I assumed Dan was target practicing. He knew we had a brick of bullets containing five hundred shots. We had an ample amount of bullets, but it wasn't necessary for him to practice shooting on this hike.

I thought about what I would say to him once he was back. How I should let him know to keep his shooting to a minimum, only firing when we were in need. It wasn't long before I got over the idea of Dan's needless shooting and enjoyed the moment, losing myself in thoughts. This has to be the ultimate father-son wilderness experience, of all time.

Most ventures resembling mine are passed down through legend. Children often only hear of adventures, but we were doing this together. I felt proud and wore a beaming smile from ear to ear. Reality soon set in; I was well aware that we had a long mission ahead of us. Seeing the distant haze of the horizon, looking at the miles and miles that lay ahead, I quickly snapped back my composure.

"I shot them, Dad. Now you get to cook them." I looked up at Dan, as he made his way back into camp. "Just kidding," he said with a wink.

"Yeah, sure what were you shooting at?"

Dan dropped twelve Bohemian Cedar waxwings to the ground. (They are small song birds).

"Well, I'll be darned!" They were the size of robins.

"We're eating fresh meat tonight, Dad!" We had never eaten small birds before, but right then, they looked delicious. I will always remember Dan's broad smile as he fried the birds.

They were so good, we ate the bones too.

"Never again will I question how many times you fire a gun, Dan."

This meal made our day complete. We retired to the tent for the night, and Dan went about killing the mosquitoes.

CHAPTER NINE: DAY 7

July 10, 1985

"How many miles do you think we will go today, Dad?" We were looking off at the distant horizon, contemplating the trek ahead.

"We have some high ground to cross but a couple of valley crossings too. There are alder thickets at the base of the hills, which will slow us down. Conservatively, I would say five or six miles."

"Dad, let me be the point man today. Maybe I can set a faster pace."

"Sure, Dan. From here, we need to follow this ridge until it drops off. We will head down to the valley, then up the next hill. See them from here? I'll try and keep up with you."

That being said, Dan proudly led the charge. We were off and away. We had gone a mere 150 feet before we were surrounded by woods again.

A little while later, as we were headed up a slight rise, Dan called out to me from near the top of the hill. "Dad, I have something to show you."

"What's that?" Dan was pointing. "Looks man-made, Dan." It was shaped like a tripod, twelve feet tall, and was made out of tree poles. Whatever it was, it had been here a long time by the look of the wood. Once I reached the tripod and could see it up close, I recognized it for what it was.

It was a land survey monument marker. The wood pole tripod was built over the monument so it could be easily located when it was needed. An army helicopter survey crew made this when they mapped Alaska, placing one every six miles. This made townships that are six square miles in size. This marker was located in the corner where four of the township's corners met. These markers have a two-foot-long rod anchored to the pole. The rods are topped with brass for longevity and marked with a compass rose. Also on these markers: the date it was placed, the elevation, and the latitude/longitude of the location. This is done for the surveyors to work from. From these monuments, surveyors are able to measure and map any future developments. A helicopter crew will use a map to locate these markers in order to complete any survey project they may have.

This particular marker was signed the Army Corp of Engineer Company and dated 1942. I took out a knife, and we carved our names and the date (7/10/85) on this brass button as well. "This brass stake and tripod pole is as old as I am, Dan. I was born in 1942. This is a historic site, we're most likely the first people here since the army map builders were in '42."

When Dan and I were finished, Dan took point, leading the way again. In this area, there were a lot of well used moose trails. One was headed off in the same direction we were traveling. Dan followed this moose path.

This area had more signs of moose than any I have ever seen. It was like a well-used barnyard. There was an abundance of moose trails, leading all over. The ground was dry but retained enough moisture for willows to grow. The paths worked their way around the willows, like it was a garden of feeding stations. The moose had kept these trimmed back like a gardener pruning his trees. They didn't eat the trees to the nubbin, but rather, they harvested only the succulent new growth.

There were moose footprints as big as an elephant's. Not only a single moose of that size, but several. To hunt and harvest moose here would take a big helicopter. I estimate a single moose could weigh an easy two thousand pounds, after it is field dressed.

Only an ignorant fool would drop a moose any distance from a river or lake. There is so much meat in a moose, it takes a plane or a boat to carry it any distance. These moose were safe from man, and I am sure any pack of wolves had great respect for them.

One hour had passed, and we still had not dropped down to the valley. "Dad, Dad! Look, another tripod!"

Knowing we had not traveled six miles, a weak feeling came over me. "Dan! Read the button."

When he did, there was a look of astonishment on his face, and his body language showed he felt defeated. "How can that be, how?" Dan just could not accept that he had just led us in a two-hour-long circle and was completely perplexed. I had been following Dan's heels, bent over, just following along behind, doing my best to keep up.

We had spent the last hour traveling in a full, twisted circle. If it had not been for that tripod, a man-made landmark, we might have been forever lost to wander the land. Or so it felt at that moment. We had been lost for an hour, without even realizing it.

"Dan, you just had lesson in getting lost. It could have been worse. We might have been confused for a day or so, but not lost." I couldn't help but laugh out loud.

"But how? The sun is up there, and there's not a cloud in the sky. I went straight?" Dan asked.

"Well, Dan, this is Alaska in July. Sure the sun is shining, however, this time of year it is near its zenith most of the day and night. As you made your way, you traveled the path of least resistance, instead of aligning landmarks. Use the compass, Dan. Ahem! You weaved, twisted, and made a straight line for an hour. All while making a slight curve, like the shape of the earth. Keep going straight west from here, and you end up right back where you started. I think that is how someone figured out this planet is round. Notice how you favored your right side and the land wasn't descending in elevation? Well, some instincts are best not followed. We're fortunate we came back to this tripod. This was an easy lesson, well learned."

Like a person with a hangover, Dan remained confused and completely befuddled.

"Guess I will take point, at least for a while. Now you know why I check my compass so often." I was not hard on him, and no more was said. Dan was going to have to take time to recover from this himself, unraveling his own puzzle with self-reflection.

I turned his attention to the matters at hand. Not one cross word was said between us. This had been a true test of our relationship, between father and son.

The mosquitoes were bad all the time, but there was a slight reprieve on the tops of hills, as well as in the direct sunlight. Never were we completely free of them. Their annoying sounds, the continuous buzzing, were maddening. Thankfully, we had the repellent and protective clothing to cover as needed. We were also thankful for the reprieve escaping to the tent gave us from the bugs. Dan had it down pat. He had mastered killing the pests that found their way trapped inside.

During one of our stops to rest, we found a bench-like log seat, with a supporting rest. This allowed us to keep our packs on while providing additional relief.

While we were resting, I decided to test how black my leg would become if I offered my bare skin to the mosquitoes. I wanted to see how many would land, drill, and pump the blood from one of my legs. I pulled my pant leg up and exposed my leg. I had no repellent on this part of my skin. Dan watched. It was not long before my leg was covered. There was not an eighth of an inch between the blood pumping drill rigs. One zillion mosquitoes, wing to wing, drilling and pumping for the commodity they savored.

Dan just shook his head and said, "Dad, they're full now."

"So they are. Watch this." With one hand, I plowed them flat, smashing them dead.

"Dang! Dad, that must have hurt?"

"Yes, it did, and now I have a red pant leg. Let's not do that again." It was time to apply more repellent.

The high noon temperatures reached one hundred degrees, adding to our discomfort. Having to be well covered with heavy clothing slowed down our pace even more. We would not have made it this far without all the preparations we took. This Alaskan jungle wilderness is not forgiving to those who take on her adventure. The best days for traveling in the Alaskan jungle is during the winter, through early spring. November on through to May. June through mid-August is the time when the insects rule the land.

We started our descent down off the ridge. We headed down to a thick jungle of swamp bogs. We had to fight our way through a wet buggy mess before we could climb another hill. Going down the north side of this hill was less of a challenge; it was relatively free of trees. The snow remains here for longer during the season because it is sheltered from the sun. There is also two feet deep moss covering the frozen ground of bedrock, which isn't a welcoming environment for trees to take root.

We often found water like this from the melted snow and ice, accumulating in the dips and sags of the terrain

It was on this hillside that we filled our canteens. There was a small gully flowing with melting ice and snow. Most likely this water was safe to drink as it was filtered from flowing through the mosses. We purified the water with tablets before drinking it, just to be on the safe side. It would not do for either of us to become sick from germ-filled water. The water tasted like medicine, but it was comforting to know it was pure and clean. These purification tablets saved time. They allowed us to have safe drinking water in a few minutes, rather than having to build a fire and wait for the water to come to rolling boil for twenty minutes.

After filling the canteens, we continued on down the hillside—slowly, deliberately, with caution. The thick layer of moss covering the tundra concealed many obstacles that could cause us to stumble, or even break a leg.

Upon safely reaching the bottom, we were immediately faced with the base of the next hill. There was heavily enclosed undergrowth to wiggle through, alder trees being the worst of the entanglements.

There are two different types of alder trees: pink alder heart wood and white alder heart wood. There is no difference on the outside. They look the same until you cut deep to the heart wood. When you cut into the heartwood, you will see the color. I like the pink wood for carving. My guess is that one is a male, the other is a female.

Thankfully, there were no thorns in this undergrowth, just a low-lying, clustered mass of shrubs. Wherever a limb of a shrub touched the ground cover, it would take root and sprout a new tree. This added to the mass of the entangled puzzle.

We had to chop our way through, using our Estwing hand ax before gaining an upward ascent. When the chopping was done, we found ourselves in a mix of white birch and spruce. It was always a great relief not to be crawling and chopping, pulling or pushing.

The dark forest offered an intermission of cooler temperatures. We still had to keep on the head nets, gloves, and light jackets. The shade didn't keep the bugs from their constant assault.

Even though the shade was cooler, it was still plenty hot. We had to drink a lot of water to avoid dehydration. Water is to people, like oil is to machines. Water is the most important element for human survival. It helps keep your body from overheating, along with all its other benefits—like staying alive.

As we worked our way closer to the top, light started filtering through. "Not much farther, Dan. The going will become easier soon. When we reach the top, we will go to the right, heading northeast. I want to take advantage of the easier traveling in the more spacious hilltop, until we reach the end of the ridgeline. The ridge, as it appears on the map, is probably three miles long."

It was a good feeling to reach the top and enjoy the expanded view that less foliage offered. The moose seemed to be enjoying this area too. Moose trails were everywhere. We decided to follow the trails, but to check the compass often. Just because a trail looked to lead the right way, didn't make it so. The compass would keep us on track.

Making good time, we reached the area where we wanted to descend the hill. This area was abundant in black basalt, a cubic-shaped rock.

It was getting later in the day, so I had to decide if we should press on or stop for the night. If we continued without stopping, we would have to make camp somewhere down in the thick, dark jungle. I did not favor that idea. "Dan, we camp here for tonight and press forward tomorrow."

Dan was all for camping near this high rocky hilltop. Working as a father-son team, it was not long before we had camp set up. This entire journey was all about teamwork. There was never a harsh word spoken between us; we had mutual respect. There was a real effort on my part to show confidence and have a decisive and positive attitude at all times. After all, we were in this journey together. To have doubts, or show panic, was not in the plan. Dan was full of questions like: What if? How far? When? Are we going to have to walk back the way we came in?

I tried to make sure I always had a good answer, mainly to reinstate his confidence in me. Even though I answered all of his questions, there were times when I didn't truly know the answer myself. Some obstacles had to be confronted first before the answer would come to me. Of one thing I was always sure: no matter what problems should arise, I would find a solution. For I truly believe we had a guardian angel guiding us on this journey. I knew how to listen to my sixth sense, to search my feelings for the answer, to meditate.

Even though we were camped out in the open, the mosquitoes were very bad at this site. There was a lack of wind to keep them subdued. It seemed we had picked the hottest time of day to make camp. Tomorrow morning would be a better time to travel, getting an early start in the cool morning hours.

I want to add something about mosquito head nets. There is no need for camouflaged head nets. This was a mistake I learned the hard way. They are very difficult to see out of, making it dangerous when traveling over rough terrain.

Dan had a very unique way of killing mosquitoes trapped inside his head net. He would simply inhale them, and swallow them whole, with a devilish glee in his eyes.

Dan inhaling the mosquitoes that were trapped in his head net

Daniel had this mosquito-killing method perfected. He would open his mouth, and if the mosquitoes did not fly in, he would just draw in air as they hovered in front of his mouth. It was his way of getting even, perhaps. Or maybe he was trying to recapture some of his blood. It also could have been one too many had bit him in the head. In any case, it was a way to make light of the otherwise horribly annoying situation.

So far, the mosquitoes in Alaska don't carry any diseases or illness, like malaria or sleeping sickness. The only thing to fear from the mosquitoes is being eaten alive, which could happen. They are as big as birds here in Alaska. Whatever you do, don't let one land on each shoulder at the same time. They will pick you up and carry you off to their young, hungry children.

From our new camp's vantage point, we could look back and see where our last camp was. This was over a distance of maybe four miles. Certainly no farther.

After turning in for the night, Dan had his fun killing the remaining mosquitoes within the tent.

"We're running low on water, Dad!"

I checked the topographic map. There was a line representing a likely water source not far from our current location. "Okay, there should be another water source less than one mile ahead."

CHAPTER TEN: DAY 8

July 11, 1985

It was going to be another hot day. Dry weather was better than wet, so we weren't complaining. After a pancake breakfast, the tent was taken down, rolled up, loaded up, and we moved on. It was a slow descent down the steep hillside. We traveled at an angle to lessen the risk of one of us tumbling. As we traveled toward the north, the forest began to open up again.

The ground was covered with moss and rotting wood. Walking on the moss was always a bit surprising. It was like stepping on a lumpy mattress.

We both wore brand-new Vietnam jungle combat boots. They gave us good traction and ankle support. The boots had a reinforced canvas, with weep drain holes. Despite the quality of our boots, the stress and strain on my boots from traveling through this tundra moss took a toll. At the bottom of this hill, I found a hump to sit on while I removed my left boot.

"What's the problem, Dad?"

"That steep hillside walk ripped out the side of my boot, right by the arch where the reinforced canvas is joined to the bottom. Dan, do you have the backpack cord?"

"Yup! Coming right up, Dad!" This cord was a roll of carpenter's chalk line. I used a length of this cord to hold the upper part of the boot to the bottom rubber sole, in order to prevent it from becoming worse. I was sure glad we brought that cord.

My method for fixing my boot

The hill we were about to climb was 1,700 feet, according to the topographic map. Going around this pointed hill would have been a shorter distance. However, the jungle at its base would have taken us at least two days to fight through.

Growing on the upper portion of this hill were large white spruce of massive sizes. These trees were ideal for house logs, and there was enough timber to build a log home.

Before we could reach the upper part of this hill, we had to get through the tangled brush at the base. The going was tough. There was a lot of chopping, wiggling, climbing over and under fallen trees. Eventually, we reached easier ground to hike through. To travel all the way around this hill through this mess would have been more trouble than it was worth.

Once we were out of the heavy undergrowth, we knew we would be able to gain some distance. We could now rest a bit easier, knowing what was behind us. Going up and over was proving to be the best choice.

It was after we punched beyond this entangled base that I noticed my $23 Estwing, leather bound hand ax was missing. The holster was busted. Turns out the cases were made rather cheaply. The case was sturdy enough for normal use, but not for this trip.

The ax was top of the line, but the case wasn't made to handle this type of abuse. I removed my pack and walked back a ways, just in case the lost ax could be easily found. I didn't want to spend much time looking for it. I could have spent days looking for it, and walked away empty-handed. I used the metal detector to assist, but even with that, I could not find it. Time was a more valuable treasure. I turned back to rejoin Dan and push on.

Estwing leather-bound hand ax

Somewhere out there is a fine, Estwing hand ax. This was a lesson to be alert and aware of the inventory that hung on us.

This was the first time we were not on rock. Instead, there was silt beneath the moss. It was like dust, gray in color, but abrasive like fine polishing grit. Upon further examination, I came to the conclusion it was volcanic ash.

I never took the time to dig down but assumed there was a stone hill under this ash, as were the other hills we had crossed over. We were on the edge of an ash fall made by a violent erupting volcano from billions of years ago.

No wonder the trees looked healthier in this area; they had a better root system, ash-rich soil, and drainage. That is why the birch and white spruce mix was prevalent. These trees were larger than the ones we had thus far encountered. Black spruce, on the other hand, likes the wetter permafrost areas, which is why it was abundant on the lowlands.

Our progress uphill was going well. While it was a task to find footholds, and the climb was arduous, we were making good progress. The hill was steep, and at times I found myself having to hold on to trees to pull myself up. Dan was some distance ahead, yet in sight. He was doing great leading the way and forging a route. We had made it a fair distance uphill when Dan turned and said, "I see the top, Dad. There's light up ahead."

"Can't be, Dan. This is the highest hill around, are you sure?"

"Yup. It looks like the hilltop is rounding off and the trees are thinning out."

Suddenly, like a marine about to plant a battle field flag, he got a burst of energy and scrambled up on out of sight. Shortly after, I heard a loud groan. "*Oh no*! Rats!"

I made my way up to Dan. The disappointing body language Dan had was understandable. We were not at the top, but on a plateau shelf on the hill. We had all of what we had climbed thus far in height yet to conquer. The makeup of the forest was the same. There was only a short, flat plateau to cross before we were back on a steep hill. There was no daylight, or sign of the top in sight.

We continued to push forward. After a bit of travel, Dan once again saw light and hurried forward. It was another plateau on the hill; our climb was not over. After three more times experiencing this scenario, I was confident we would soon summit the top. Just to be sure, I sent Dan on ahead. He came back and shouted, "We're here!" Because of the tree cover, we could only see to the north and the west. We knew where we were; it didn't matter if we couldn't see every direction.

To the west of our location was the Kuskokwim Mountain range. It felt close in proximity, but looked barren of life. We were headed in a more northern direction, which looked green and full of life. "Open country!" Dan loudly proclaimed. Open country meant there were no trees, only grasses.

"Let me have a look, Dan. True, it is open country, but we are not headed that way."

"Rats!" Dan said.

I pointed out the path of our route to Dan.

"Another jungle, huh, Dad?"

"Looks like it. With a lot of swamp land to find our way around, to boot. We have to cross that vast bottom to get to those hills way yonder. At least part of the trip will be easier."

"Yeah! I'm headed down," Dan said. Traveling down was almost fun. Of course, that kind of thinking could get us into trouble. Therefore, I continued carefully on down but at a little quicker pace. Going downhill was definitely less work and less effort.

Our drinking water was running low, so we headed in search of clues that would lead us to a water source. Dan was the first to hear running water.

It was hidden from view, but it was getting louder—telling us we were close. It seemed to be coming down a narrow groove in the side hill. Dan honed in on the sound of gushing water, like a heat-seeking missile.

There it was, coming right out of a stone wall. Water shooting straight out of the wall for a good two feet from the pressure, before gravity pulled it down. The artesian water stream was two inches across, before it fell eight feet down into a basin. I watched it spilling over the basin and then seeping back into the ground.

The water was ice-cold, barely above freezing temperatures. The force of the stream remained at a constant. By the look of it, it has been flowing here since the beginning of time. This was on the dark side of the mountain and eight feet above the valley floor. This 1,700 feet mountain we had just come down from had trapped water in its belly. The water found escape from its rocky prison and spewed forth proudly, aggressively seeking its unknown destination. This stream was like the story of Moses in the Bible. This flowing water had enough force, it could have been used to make electricity and supply a home with a forever water source.

This water was the best I have ever tasted. No stink to it, only clear, cold, pure water. Someday I would like to revisit this site. Sadly, I did not take a photo of the flowing stream of water. I do have a photo of the level ground it landed on and dispersed into. This flowing force was concealed behind thick shrubs and trees. I would have had to do a lot of clearing for a good photo. In hindsight, I should have.

This water gave us a refreshing opportunity to clean up a little. However, it was too cold for a full-on shower. The cool air in this immediate area lessened the number of mosquitoes present, allowing us to remove the head nets. It was very invigorating washing in ice-cold water and brushing our teeth.

Dan even shampooed his hair, looking all pretty. For whom, I do not know, but he felt better. The backpacker's signal mirror was used.

We had the running water; now we just needed the sink. Dan even endured the cold water pouring on his head to rinse the shampoo out. I would have gotten a brain freeze. He just grinned and smiled. Dan is the sort of person who would laugh in the face of evil.

"Dad!" Dan said.

"What?"

"Dad, the right side of your head looks like raw hamburger."

I used the mirror to inspect myself, and with my hand, I felt the damage to the side of my head near my temple. What had happened was apparent. My head net had been up against my temple, and the mosquitoes had their way with me. The whole right half of my head is paralyzed due to the bullet wound I received in 1977. I had not felt a single thing.

The damage was serious and needed to be tended to or infection would take over. It was a two-inch area of bloody, raw flesh. "It's first aid time, Dad!" We treated it like a burn, applying burn ointment, after thoroughly washing with that cold, clean, running water.

Notice the raw skin on my right temple

"A guardian angel is with us, Dad." Thankfully, I did not feel the cold water. This self-flowing water was truly a blessing. Had this raw flesh not been found, it could have very well become infected. This wasn't the first time my careful preparations paid off. I was grateful to have a full medical kit to treat my wound. From this point forward, we were careful to make sure our nets did not come close to our skin.

We rested for a bit, filling up on water, drinking until we had our fill. We filled the canteens and moved on to complete the day. It was always a hard go in the bottom lands; this day would be no different.

We had spent the next few hours hacking our way forward when a gleam of light appeared up ahead. We were drawn toward it, like moths to a flame. "Well look at that, Dad! Neat huh?"

We had come upon a marshy area, filled with tall water grasses. It looked like a jungle lagoon deep within the forest. An eerie feeling overcame me while standing on the edge of this hidden lagoon. It felt as though we had gone two million years back in time.

There was an air of expectation, as though any moment an ancient monster would raise its head above the misty lagoon. This lagoon had a solid bank; dry land reached right to the water's edge. This seemed very unusual to me. I used a long pole to probe the ground. I pushed the pole down sixteen feet, but could not feel the bottom.

"I think this is a warm spring, Dan. The kind that never freezes." Alaska is known for hot springs. They are not always hot, but warm enough to keep from freezing over. I am sure this pond is one such hot spring.

I wish I'd had the time and equipment to drag the depths for bones. I'm sure there is a treasure trove of history down there. This marshy area could easily be hidden from aerial view. It may have stayed forever unknown, if we hadn't chanced upon it. "Dan, we're very fortunate to have come across this."

"It's water detour time, Dad!"

"Yup!" Luckily, this was a contained round lagoon, not a lake-sized water source. "We can walk around this. Let's hope we don't run into a big marsh we have to go around."

We were still in the jungle, using a compass to guide our way. It wasn't much fun, but at times it was very interesting indeed. "I hear running water, Dad!"

"Good. On the map, there's a creek ahead, so we're making some headway." The creek had running water, but was so overfilled with fallen trees, we could walk over it on the dead falls. It was a trench-size rushing creek—the kind of creek that disappears into the undergrowth, and underground.

Dan was far up ahead of me, but I lingered, taking my time. Wearing this heavy backpack, and crossing a treacherous creek, made for a dangerous combination. Things could quickly go wrong, like falling upside down in the water and getting trapped by my heavy pack. I didn't fancy drowning in such a way.

I heard Dan yell out an urgent call. I immediately sprang into action. When hiking in the wilderness, an urgent call could mean life or death. There was no time to yell for more information.

A responsive, timely reaction could save a life. Dan was yelling, "Dad! Hurry up! Come quick!" A thousand thoughts ran through my mind as I hurried toward Dan. He looked okay! But what was he standing in?

"Is it a clearing? Dad...what is this?"

"It's a bloody miracle, that's what it is, Dan! Several years ago, a big Caterpillar bulldozer that had wide track pads for winter traveling was driven through here. It was probably done in the winter months. Perhaps during March, when the days were long, but before the top layer of ground began to thaw. It could have been through this area as long ago as 1942. Did you know the airstrip on Lake Minchumina was built by a Caterpillar dozer, Dan? The Caterpillar dozer had to have been walked into this remote location, going well over 150 miles, way back when. From where, I could only guess. Somewhere from the Parks Highway, or the Kuskokwim Mountain range, is my best estimate."

Over time, the undergrowth reclaimed most of the trail that was made, but there were still areas that remained cleared. Traveling in the winter with the dozer, there would have been no real damage to the countryside, except for the trees it pushed over.

"In any case, Dan, there truly is a guardian angel watching over us."

"What do you mean, Dad?"

"Well, look at this for a moment. The track pads from the Caterpillar bulldozer packed down a path, leading the way we're headed. It is only by chance you came across this path. It is likely that this exposed trail will be hidden by willows in a short distance. We lucked out in finding this exposed portion of the trail. We found another piece of history, Dan, one we easily could have overlooked."

Looking toward the heavens, I said, "Thank you, God!"

I turned to Dan. "We could have been off by twenty feet or less and never saw this. Now let's make use of the time this trail will save us."

We followed this Caterpillar trail for a long ways. It took us through some of the thickest, low-lying undergrowth of our hike. If I had to guess the two feet wide pads must have come from a D-8 Caterpillar bulldozer, with extra-wide winter pads installed.

We could clearly see the imprints from the dozer. It was as if they were made yesterday. We knew that wasn't the case, as the trees and shrubs that grew back over the trail were at least forty years old. The trees that were felled when the trail was originally made had either rotted away or were caught up hanging on nearby trees.

I could see that the moose used the tracks to their advantage— eating the willows that grew nearby, leaving the trail cleared of forest growth up to head height. There were two paths created by the dozer tracks, one more used than the other.

I figure the moose favored one track more than the other because there was more wood to eat in the well-used path. The Cat trail eventually broke into a very large area. It was approximately 260 acres of meadow and hassocks.

This open area could have been created when it was snow dragged flat, in order for an otter airplane to land, or even a big chopper. I suspect it was used to resupply the trailblazers, and the machinery brought in to make the trail, with fuel, food, and any other needs. A Caterpillar train pulling sleds would have been needed to flatten this big of an area. This was done to make the airfield during WWII, sometime during the early '40s.

Someday, there will be a road leading from the Parks Highway south of Nenana, up to Lake Minchumina, and onto Nome. There will be a need for the road to access the many resources the Alaskan wilderness has to offer, to support the growing population. There may even be a railroad to Russia someday. I have already seen the beginning stages of my prediction.

It was time to find a place to make camp, but where? This was a hassock, and wetlands are no-man's-land. It was the course I had set; we had to cut across some of it. Hassocks are marshy areas, where marsh plants and grasses grow in a column. They form where there is standing water on top of the permafrost.

Hassocks are a hiker's nightmare. They cannot be stepped on, unless one is of a large diameter size. Most are narrow and have to be straddled, or walked around. They don't form in any particular pattern, so they serve as a big maze.

This area seemed to be the home for sparrow hawks, which live on rodents and weasels. The problem we had was it was nearing two o'clock in the morning, there was still daylight, but it was fading fast. We needed to find a round enough hummock to set our tent upon, to get some sleep. We looked all about for that round spot for the tent. "Over here, Dad!"

"Not much, Dan, but it will have to do."

The self-supporting tent barely fit on this big hummock. Inside our tent, there was a lump in the center that we circled our bodies around, sleeping in a curve. All night, there were noises outside of water lapping, and of moose walking nearby. The moose made a sucking sound when their big feet sunk in the marshy land and when they lifted them up to take another. It was music to our ears, and we went fast to sleep.

CHAPTER ELEVEN: DAY 9 AND 10

July 12–13, 1985

"This is not your perfect campsite, huh, Dad?"

"No, but it might make a good duck blind."

We had entered into a new kind of valley. It was more open than any before it. There were some hummocks, and dead, dry black spruce, barren of limbs. This was the only vegetation in this area. Apparently, the ground had become too wet for the spruce that used to grow here. The spruce had died off, leaving behind only the pole of their trunks. Killdeer birds favored this country.

Our day was fairly uneventful. We did gain about eight miles headway; it was one of our better days.

At the day's end, we set up camp on a sandbar that was located on a small creek, with spruce trees growing on its higher bank. The creek provided drainage for the trees to grow. Wet ground does not make for healthy trees. Creeks are easily seen from great distances because of the tall trees growing along their banks. Trees growing near sources of water have a better chance of surviving a wildfire.

The tundra was too wet and looked like it had been burned off several years ago. There was no dead wood on the ground; it had rotted away. Only a few dead trunks were left standing.

The dry sandbar made for a good campsite. There were no worries of a campfire getting out of control; water was close by.

Before we put the tent up, I showed Dan how to dig in the sand. We dug out shallow depressions where our hips would be while we were sleeping, for comfort. There was no moss padding here. "Good idea, Dad!"

"Experience, Dan, experience! Stick with me, and you will learn."

After supper, we looked back to review the distance we had traveled. We had come a long ways. This was no hilltop, but it still offered a view. We could see a long distance in every direction. We had our typical campfire talks about our trek and everything that we had overcome. Dan was now a veteran hiker.

We still had miles to go, but we felt confident now. With continued caution, we would be fine. We both decided it was time to turn in and get some sleep. After long hard hours of hiking, sleep was a welcome comfort. "Goodnight, Dan. See you in the morning." Or so I had planned.

Our night's sleep was rudely interrupted around 2:00 a.m. We had been soundly sleeping, but that suddenly changed.

"Dad, Dad! Is that you?"

I woke with a lurch. "*Shut up! I am trying to get some bleep bleep sleep, dang it!*" I rolled over and went back to sleep. So did Dan.

In the morning, the first thought that popped in my mind was of Dan waking me up the previous night. Was he having a bad dream, or what? I had to ask, "Dan, about last night. Sorry I yelled at you."

"That's okay, Dad. Whatever it was, your loud angry voice chased it off."

"What do you mean?"

"Well, I was sound asleep when I was suddenly woken up. Something was pushing me from the outside of the tent. I was pushed over a good six inches. I thought it was you. When you answered my question, I got real scared, but only for a moment because whatever was pushing me didn't want anything to do with you. It went away when you started yelling, so I went back to sleep."

My eyebrows rose. "Let's check this out. We're on a sandbar. There should be tracks."

"*Holy cow!*" we both exclaimed.

"Dan, my son, we are very lucky. Last night we were visited by—by the size of these tracks—*a big, mean grizzly bear*!"

"Maybe so, Dad, but you're meaner," Dan said with a laugh.

The paw prints were six and a half inches wide, by ten and a half inches long, with three inch claws extending from the toes. This grizzly had nuzzled Dan over, then heard my loud angry voice and ran off scared.

Leaving the creek, we had to travel on a low, wide, gradually sloping hillside, which drained into this same creek. It was looking to be an easy walk. Dan was in the lead, moving right along, when he turned to me and said, "Dad, what's this?"

"It seems to be an old creek filled in with moss."

Upon further investigation, I discovered it was not a creek. On this long sloping hillside, there was a soggy strip where moss was growing. It was as though there was a crack in the ground, which had filled in with soaking wet moss. It was very odd and very much out of place. Everywhere else, there were dry hills of burned off trees. The wet area had no banks; it was even to ground level. It was about two miles long, all two miles full of saturated ground cover.

This drainage area had a few water puddles, low green moss, and algae growth. There was also six-inch high water grasses growing in it. This wet area was anywhere from eight to sixteen feet wide. Growing occasionally throughout the area were spindly tamarack trees, which had taken hold on clumps of firmer growing moss.

Unfortunately, there were no other trees in this area. Had there been even one, we could have used it to cross over the swampy area, laying it across the ground to make a bridge. I could tell this soggy slope was not a normal wet spot. At first glance, it didn't appear to present much of an obstacle. I thought it might be just a wet crossing, but nothing more.

Going around would mean traveling at least a mile either direction. It was like looking over a crevasse, contemplating a jump across so we could quickly be on our way. Dan wanted to charge across this ground; he was not afraid of getting a little wet. Holding Dan back was like trying to hold a horse that smelled water after a long dry spell on the range. Poking into it with a slender pole, I found it to be *quicksand*! I could not feel the bottom with my pole. It was all thick, stinking, sucking muck. "That's that, Dan. We have to go around."

"But that will mean hours of extra work, Dad!"

"Sorry, Dan, but we can't go across that quicksand. We would just sink and be stuck if we tried."

I was ready to walk around, going up to higher ground where there should be solid turf to cross. I saw a movement from the corner of my eye in this muck. I focused my eye where I saw the movement, searching for what had caused it.

There were small holes, about one inch in diameter, here and there in the thin moss cover. I had not noticed them before. "Watch, Dan. There's something living in them holes."

We stood still, staring. A ten-inch-long snake slithered quickly from one hole to another. I noticed a second snake in a different spot. These snakes had round heads, not blunt-shaped. This told me that they most likely had no fangs like those on a rattler. We saw three snakes in all. They moved extremely fast, swiftly darting to their next destination. All of them were around the same length, eight to ten inches.

The snakes were reddish in color, although the color could have come from the muck they lived in. I wondered how a snake could be living here, in the center of Alaska, with such a cold climate.

I put my hand in this mucky, watery quicksand and discovered it was warm. It was certainly not cold like other wet spots and water streams, which we had encountered. That explained things. These snakes had their own warm environment to thrive in.

Had I known at the time that there have been no recordings of snakes in the center of Alaska, I would have captured one and put my name on the species.

We turned back to the task at hand. It's too bad we didn't have a film crew following us. The events that followed would have made for a great movie.

Dan found a place where the wet ground was narrower. There was a small tree in the middle of this area, but it wasn't much more than a clump.

"Let me try, Dad."

"Take your pack off, and come over here." I tied a fifty-foot rope under his arms. I could have ordered Dan to follow me around this quicksand seep, but there are some things in life best learned the hard way. All the same, I was not about to lose my son in this lesson.

Dan took his first step, sank some right off, but not too deep. He took his next step and sank more. He was a little deeper, but still okay. Each move forward, he sank more. He was now in well over his knees. It was like seeing Dan walk down a set of steps, if each step was eight inches deep. "Can you feel bottom?"

"There is none, only mushy muck."

"Turn back, Dan. Give it up."

"I can make it, Dad. I am nearly to that tree."

With every move, Dan started sinking faster and faster. It became more of a struggle just trying to move. (Ever see quicksand at work? It is not pretty.) Dan turned back facing me, up to his armpits in the muck. He was stuck, and sinking.

Me pulling Dan out of the quicksand

Dan was out of my reach, but thanks to the Lord, he had a rope tied under his arms. I was not quick in pulling him out; the lesson was not done. Dan looked up at me, still sinking inch by inch. His arms were now hugging the mucks surface, and soon it would pull him in all the way.

About this time, Dan said, "*Pull, Dad!*" His voice was beginning to sound panicky. "*Pull now, now!*"

Dan was firmly stuck. Pulling him was like pulling up an anchor stuck to the bottom in heavy mud.

Dan held fast to the rope, and I pulled with all my might. Slowly, like pulling out a fence post, he was moving upward. He was leaning like a water skier coming up on the surface. Finally, he was on top of the muck. I dragged him back to solid ground.

"Peeuee, you stink something God awful, Dan."

Dan had that quirky smile from ear to ear, glad to be back on solid ground again. "Well, Dad, I learned a new lesson today."

"That you did, Dan, that you did. Now though you're going to have to run back on down to the creek and jump in clothes and all. You smell like rotten bear bait. I will wait here and look for more snakes."

It was frustrating to Dan that a long, but narrow, seeping wet spot could stop our progress. However, after this quicksand experience, he was happy to walk around. This indeed was an adventurous journey.

Now that we were back on our way, we went to see what was over the next ridge. We couldn't wait to leave this area of dead forest.

A wildfire had raged through here in the past. What was left behind were sticks, ashes, and tree stumps. Most of the dead fallen trees had rotted away. This fire must have happened a long time ago. Walking was fairly easy, except for navigating over some rotting logs and weaving around new growth. This old burn painted a picture of how the fire had behaved. Walking through it, we could see the path of nature's carnage.

Once we reached the ridge top, we could see where the force of the fire had rushed up both sides of this hill. It was like a giant bonfire, the flames coming together, slaughtering everything in its path. The dead trees leaned against each other. It was as though the trees had found comfort in each other while they died a horrible, fiery death. It had been an extremely hot fire of hurricane force.

Destruction left behind from a wildfire

Nothing was left standing, except for the dried out, barren, lifeless logs. The trees were soldiers supporting each other for eternity in death. What once was a forest was now completely void of life—a flora and fauna graveyard.

Something most people aren't aware of is that a wildfire does not often burn green trees to ash. Typical fires only burn the dry fuels while killing the green trees to fall and rot later. It's common for controlled fires to be set, in order to burn away the dead ground fuels. These are done during damp mornings, when there is little to no wind in the weather service report.

Clearing out the fire-tinder underbrush is a lifesaving measure for any forest. Back fires are done this way to take away the fuels that a forest fire would feed on, forcing the oncoming monsters to burn itself out.

This photo is of a controlled burn. The photo was taken a week after the burn was set. The controlled burn was done in the late of night and burned into the early morning before dawn. A controlled burn takes several hours to complete, so it's best done while the humidity is high and not a breeze is blowing. The firefighters snuff out the fires as the fuels are burned away.

A raging, out of control wildfire is brought to a halt when it reaches the man-made barrier. With no food to consume, the fire starves into oblivion.

"It looks like we found open country, Dan. We're back up on high ground."

Continuing on, we crested another hill of a higher elevation. From this point, we had our first good view of our destination.

"It's time to breakout the maps, Dan." Using the compass, maps, and landmarks, we located ourselves once again on the map. "We're here, and that big lake north of us is here on the map. According to the map, we are eight air miles away from that lake. It appears to be a good-sized lake, about one mile in diameter. That is our final destination. Now look at the last lake on the left. Four miles left of that lake is our aiming point. That is the first area I want to see, so I can decide if it's suitable for my needs. If you look to the right, at the highest hill on the western face, which is the second place I want to scout out. On the top of that hill is my third and final choice for us to inspect. We're a lot closer than we were July 4."

"Our packs are lighter too, Dad."

"How are we doing on food, Dan? Do we have enough to make it through our trip?"

"It will be close. Our freeze-dried steak supply and our other foods are getting low. Don't worry. The wild berries are ready to eat. They are a little green, but still edible. We also have fresh meat we can shoot, like grouse. We should be okay. Dad, look over on the far shoreline of that lake. What do you make that out to be?"

"Yeah, I see it. There are some sixty-four claims over there, scattered around all the lakes, and other places on the thirty thousand acres. There are a number of people on that lake. Someone should be home. What we're seeing is a structure. It appears to be a tall, white Indian lodge. Someday we will make it there."

"*Yeah!*" Dan shouted.

"There will be planes, dogs, kids, boats, cabins, and good cooking. From that lake, or one of the other four, we will hop on a flight back to Fairbanks."

From here, we could see the lakes that were our final target

Having the end in sight gave us a new rush of energy and encouragement. We both felt a renewing of vigor, eager to succeed in our goal. We made camp that night on this high ground, with a beautiful panoramic view of my future homestead. Lord willing, a spot of land would speak to my heart. "Like a lasting relationship, Dan, if there is land out there meant for me, the feelings will be mutual."

CHAPTER TWELVE: DAY 11

July 14, 1985

The time had come for the wild berries to start making an appearance. We were able to eat a good portion of our diet off the land. Even though most of the berries were still green, we didn't mind. The berries were zestful, like green apples. Currants and cloudberries were abundant.

Cloudberry is raspberry plant that grows low to the ground, with large leaves. When cloudberries mature, they are red to orange in color and the size of your thumb. Each plant has only one berry. Cloudberries can be found on northern moss-covered slopes, as well as in the shaded bottomlands.

Currants are very tasty. The plants grow knee-high in clusters, and the berries hang in a row. They can be found in the sheltered woods, on hillsides, or most anywhere. There are two kinds of currants. One tastes bad, and I think they are poisonous. I call those skunk berries because they stink so badly.

You can differentiate between the good currants and the bad ones by their appearance. The bad ones are fuzzy while the good ones are smooth. It is very easy to see the difference. If you pick them too fast, you might get them confused.

At first glance, they look the same. Check your berry book to be sure; I am no expert. I only have my personal experience in knowing the difference between the two berries. My rule is anything that tastes bad, is bad. Or at least this holds true for me.

Whenever we could, we picked and ate the cloudberries. Some areas were abundant with them. I recall one place in particular that was so full of berries, we had no problem eating our fill. We would eat the currants as we traveled, but Dan would also store them for us to eat later when we made camp. We had run out of the raisins we brought for snacking, so the currants were a blessing.

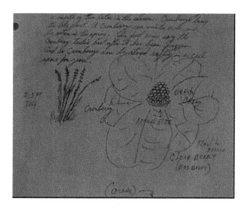

My depiction of cloudberry plants and their berries

We still had plenty of the drink mix Tang, which Dan loved. He would wet his fingers and jam them into the Tang. That was his favorite way to get his Tang, although we also mixed it in our canteen water. Tang was a great help in getting us to drink plenty of water. (See! We were not hurting.)

We had currants each night before we went to sleep, thanks to Dan. We spent a good portion of our day picking and eating berries, as we traveled along. What we needed most though was water. Traveling up on the ridgeline was easier ground to traverse, but we needed to descend to a lower elevation to find a water source. Ice could be found in the shaded mossy areas, but up here it was just hot and dry.

Our traveling had led us to an old burn in the forest, and it was perhaps the worst burned area we had seen thus far. In the time since the fire moved through this area, the new growth had reached a maturity where the tree trunks had grown to two inches in diameter. The thick new growth mixed with the fallen trees, roots sticking in all directions. This made for a three-dimensional jigsaw puzzle for us to traverse. It was a daytime nightmare!

Like bulldozers, we put our backs into plowing our way across this difficult terrain. We forced our way through, climbing over and under dead falls, twisting and turning around obstacles.

After some time had passed with us pressing forward, we came to a small clearing. I decided it was a good time for us to take a rest and rehydrate. I went to reach for my canteen and said to myself, "*Oh crap!*"

Since the start of our hike, I had made sure to consistently warn Dan not to lose his two-quart canteen. He carried his canteen by slinging it over his framed backpack. I carried a mountain pack for our hike, so I strapped my two one-quart canteens securely to my army utility belt. When I reached down to grab them, I realized one was missing. Dan noticed the look on my face and asked, "What's wrong, Dad?"

"Well, first, I lost my brand-new ax. Now I lost a canteen full of precious water."

"*No*! You didn't, huh, Dad?"

"I am afraid so, Dan." Dan decided now would be a good time to remind me how I had been harping on him the entire trip about being careful not to lose his canteen. I still had one of my canteens attached to my belt, and Dan still had his two-quart canteen, so it isn't like we were totally empty-handed. However, on a hike like this, where we never knew for sure that there would be a new water source, losing a canteen and the water it could carry was dangerous.

"Maybe I can backtrack and find it!"

"Sure, Dad, do you think you can find the trail we just plowed through?" I looked behind us and had no clue as to where we had just been.

We poked around a bit to see if we could easily find it, but eventually I decided I would just have to call it a lost canteen.

Now we would have to be extremely careful not to overextend ourselves and need more water than we could carry. Dan put an extra grip on his big canteen, double-checking the sling.

It was not long before we faced our first test of surviving through the loss of my water canteen. Once we broke out of the tangled maze, we were able to make good time. We were back up on the ridgeline, and the sun was blazing hot. It had to be well over a hundred degrees, with not so much as a small breeze to ease our discomfort.

The foliage was wilting, hanging limp in despair from the heat. It was even too hot for the mosquitoes. Water was consuming most of my thoughts, although our supply wasn't yet dangerously low.

The scorching heat forced our bodies to sweat, the natural defense to keeping cool. The water lost from sweating had to be replaced frequently, in order to remain healthy and alert.

"Where's our guardian angel now, Dad?"

"We are okay. We still have lots of berries and water enough to get us through today. We will find water at the end of this ridge as we drop down."

We had been continually on the move for eighteen hours now. Normally, we would make camp at sites where there was a water source. Looking at my map, I was dismayed to discover the closest possible water source was over two miles away.

A water source is represented by a line on the topographic map, indicating a draw or drainage, although these water sources could always be dry, only providing drainage during the wet seasons.

Topographic maps are blessing to backpackers, and every hiker should study them well. They should be brought along on hiking adventures and kept in an easily accessible place, making sure to keep them from becoming wet. Nowadays, GPS gives pinpoint locations—a convenience I lacked, considering it was not available at that time. A good compass should also be in a backpacker's possession for backup. In order to use a cell phone, the phone needs to be within thirty miles of a cell tower.

That night was a dry camp; we had only enough water for drinking, not for cooking. We had berries for dessert, thanks to Dan, leaving a bunch to eat the next day. That night, we had our last drink of water.

"Okay, Dan! We have two options on how to proceed tomorrow. First, we could leave our camp set up so that we can travel light in search for water, then return to camp for our things.

The hottest day of our trip, you can see the plant life wilting

"Our second choice is you staying here in the tent so you can save your energy. Both of us will have to keep an ear open for three shots, signaling distress. I will flag, marking my way down the side hill east of where we are now. I plan to drop down to lower ground and hopefully find water. If we decide on this plan, I will make sure and return by noon, or thereabouts. Once I get back, we will break camp and head north on down to water."

"It is too hot for a forced march with all the weight we have to carry. I don't like the first choice, and I'm not real fond of the second choice either. We have to find water, and the second choice seems the better of the two."

CHAPTER THIRTEEN: DAY 12

July 15, 1985

This morning, our breakfast consisted of some of the currants that we had in abundance, saving some for later. The day was clear, and there was a slight breeze. We decided to go forward with plan number 2. I had to set out early, during the coolest time of day.

"Dan, it's very important to rest. Keep out of the sun by remaining in the tent. I will mark my trail by flagging it. There will always be two flags in view so you won't have to guess where my trail is. If I have trouble, I will fire my shotgun three times and wait for your one return shot. If there is no reply in a timely fashion, I will fire another three rounds. If you have to come for me, be careful not to stumble or get hurt in anyway. I will be back around noon, with or without water."

I proceeded on down, using survey tape to flag my trail, all the while craning my neck, looking for any clues of a water source. I kept my ears open for running, gurgling water. I was nearing the halfway point, and progress through the undergrowth was getting difficult. The jungle was becoming thicker. The halfway point to get back by noon was soon at hand.

I was sure there would be water downhill farther, but the plan was to be back around noon. It was becoming abundantly clear to me that this valley's floor was beyond my judgment of time, which I had set for myself. There was only one thing to do. Climb back uphill to Dan. I worked my way back up, following my flagged trail. Flagging my trail was proving to be a great help in making a quick retreat back up to Dan. It was well worth the extra work.

As I crested the hill, I could see the tent some fifty yards away. The tent looked welcoming in the bright, glaring, hot sun. I did not see Dan, so assumed he was inside keeping cool the best he could, considering the one-hundred-degree temperature outside.

All I could think was, what am I going to tell Dan? I knew our only remaining option was to make a forced march, and the sooner the better. I was in a hurry to tell Dan the news. I looked around for a place to sit, to really think about what I was going to tell Dan.

This ridge was all rock, with very little plant life, other than some scrub brush. I noticed a swell, a shallow dip on the side of this hill. Near it, I saw what looked like a round sofa cushion, made of thick moss. This mossy area was about six feet in diameter, and eighteen inches high. Thinking to myself, that looks comfortable. I decided to go over and sit on it.

Our moss-covered savior

I eased myself down on this mossy cushion, not sure if I would just sink down or hit a firmer obstacle. With my full weight on it, I found it to be very comfortable.

Almost immediately, my pants became wet. *Wet!* I stood up, turned around, and thrust my fist deep inside it. I opened my hand within this moss, grabbed a handful, and brought it out so I could examine it. The white roots of this moss were dripping wet, not just damp, but saturated…*water!*

Quickly, I set up a handkerchief filter and filled all the canteens. I made only a small hole in the moss while retrieving the water. There had to have been a hundred gallons of water in that big moss cushion.

The water tasted of moss, but I used the water purification tablets to make it safe to drink. After shaking the canteens full of water, and waiting a few minutes for the tablets to work their magic, the water was safe for us to drink.

To think we were only fifty yards from water all this time. This was a new lesson for me: water can be found on a hot, dry hilltop. Thank you, God!

Dan had no idea of the highs and lows I had just experienced in my search for water. He was waiting patiently in the tent like I had instructed him to do.

I handed a canteen to Dan for him to have a drink. Dan, without sipping or tasting, chugged some down. He gave me a funny look and said, "Wow! Dad, that water tastes like medicine and moss."

I turned to Dan to tell him the story of finding this miraculous water.

"See, Dad, our guardian angel is still with us."

"You have that right."

With the water, we prepared a late but filling breakfast. With full tummies, we loaded up and moved on. "I knew I could count on you, Dad!"

"I had help, Dan, I had help. We need to be wise and continue on with caution. It's not because of luck, Dan, that we have come this far. It is because of our careful planning and preparations, as well as the knowledge we gain each passing day. Life is an adventure. We are fortunate to be sharing this father-son wilderness adventure together.

Others will learn from us, some may even be inspired to make their own life-changing journey. Be alert, press on with pride, and live your life with no regrets."

It was a long day, but even with a late start, we were able to travel a distance of eight miles. That was our farthest progress in a single day. At last, we reached the end of this ridgetop. It rounded out at first, and then dropped steeply down, through a thick stand of trees. The sound of fast-moving water in the distance spurred us on. It was after midnight, and getting darker.

"Hurry up, Dad! Hurry up!" Dan was following close behind me as we descended the hill. We swung from tree to tree, using them to keep our balance on the steep incline. Gravity was increasing our momentum, no longer were we going for a walking pace hike. Rather, we were performing a monkey dance.

The rushing water was growing louder. We had to be close, but no creek was in sight. Reaching the creek would mean the day's end, and we could set camp up. We were excited by the sound of rushing water. At this time, we were almost free-falling downhill. We were moving so effortlessly fast. In fact, I thought we were moving more than fast enough. Until Dan once again said, "Hurry up, Dad!" *Smash! Crack!* "Ahh!"

Quick as a blink, I found myself lying on my back. My body was hanging with my arms to my sides, draped over fallen trees. My boot heels were on the ground, and white torrents of water were just six feet under me.

There I was, laying face up on top of my full pack, hat on, shotgun in one hand, metal detector in the other. The creek was narrow, but the water was gushing down this deep mountain creek. It was covered with fallen trees, and other debris, but nothing stable enough to support my full weight.

I was holding on for dear life, with my heavy pack weighing me down. If I would have fallen with my pack on in this deep mountain stream of rushing water, I would surely have drowned, or at least come close to it.

One of our dangerous close calls

The dry, dead trees were about four inches in diameter, and they were creaking and cracking. It was like they were telling me, "We can't hold you much longer." I felt the trees were getting ready to dump me into this foreboding, wet monster, with open jaws inviting my death. I did not see the humor in this situation at all.

"*This is another fine fix you got me into!* Stop laughing, and pull me out of this."

I was helpless, the full heavy pack was pulling me down bit by bit—a crack and creak at a time. My hands were busy clinging to the trees. If I fell in this fashion, it would be bad news. My head could get smashed on a rock, or I could get tangled underwater, if my grip slipped. At best, I would just get wet. Worst case, I would be pressed underwater by the force of the current and drown.

To Dan, this all looked funny. He was laughing loudly, but not for long. "Dad, do you need a hand?"

"No, Dan. This is fun! Grab your shotgun first, then the detector. Now give me a hand!"

"Thanks, Dan, I think you saved my life."

We had no time to chitchat; we needed to get on with setting up camp. We had to clear out a space for our tent, followed by putting it up. We were so used to our routine at this point, there were no instructions needed. We both understood our roles in this task.

We were now a team, and a mighty good one at that. In no time flat, we had the tent up, bedrolls laid out, and Dan had supper on the grill. It was morning when we finally went to sleep. As soon as my head hit my improvised pillow (my folded-up jacket), I was out. I didn't hear much from Dan either. Maybe it was the soothing sound of the rushing water, or maybe it was exhaustion for the day's ordeal. No matter, we were soon fast asleep.

CHAPTER FOURTEEN: DAY 13

July 16, 1985

Needless to say, this was a lazy morning. We had water, cool shade, the mosquitoes were not all that bad, and the end of the journey was close at hand.

"Okay, Dan. Today we head for the possible home site number 1. It is the first one we will encounter following this path. It's ahead maybe two to three miles. It's an unclaimed site, which I picked out after looking at the black-and-white satellite photo. It touches the mountains of the Kuskokwim range. Of the thirty thousand acres open for selection, it is located the farthest west of all the land in the settlement area. There is more land to the north, close to Wien Lake, if this site doesn't suit me."

We set our compass and headed off in a northeastern direction. Leaving the hills behind us, we began our stumbling hike through black spruce and thickets of alders. There was plenty of watery ground at the base of these hills; most were filled with hummocks. We spent a few hours traveling through this terrain, headed for our first possible homesite destination.

There were clearings in the alder groves we traversed, and it was in those clearings where we saw signs of ground squirrel mounds. Dan was in the lead, carrying the 12-gauge shotgun. "Dad, hurry on ahead!"

Dan was looking down at a fresh pile of bear crap. "It's real fresh, huh, Dad?" There were also piles of freshly dug earth made by the squirrels. "What are the tracks from, Dad?"

"They're grizzly tracks, Dan. The grizzly must have just been here."

"That bear is not too far away, huh, Dad?"

I held my hand close over the pile of crap. I could feel the heat rising from it. "I would say about two minutes ago."

"*Gee!*" Dan said. "Dad, here, you take the gun. You take point for a while." We were definitely in grizzly bear country. There were a lot of ground squirrels in this area, and those grizzly bear were pestering them to death.

Dan was following close behind now. I was in front with the 12-gauge shotgun loaded and ready for bear. I didn't quite have the heart to tell Dan the bear may come up from behind us. We were traveling tight together anyway, both of us in a high state of alert. I was ready to pump a loaded shell into the firing chamber.

As I was turning to go around an uprooted tree stump, I saw out of the corner of my eye a massive dark shape. My heart stopped beating, as I pumped a live round in the chamber and took aim. I narrowed my eye, pointed my gun, and realized it was only another uprooted tree, with moss hanging from the roots.

With my right fist, I pounded once hard on my chest to restart my heart. *Thump!*

We continued on our way, eager to leave behind that particular bear, and eager to reach our next destination. Sometime later, we found ourselves on a small rise, just short of site number 1. Using the rifle scope, I scouted the land area ahead of us. I was not impressed. There were no big trees, and the ground was too low. Things just didn't feel right. Besides, this was grizzly bear country. Well scratch that site.

"We will head northeast, Dan, crossing the bottomlands. Then we will make our way to the hill with the elevation of 1,405 feet."

The second site I wanted to check out was near the top side of this hill, facing the direction we were traveling. It was located more to the southwest, making it good for a sunset view, but it wouldn't give much view of the sun to the south.

We had been traveling for a good amount of time, and we both needed to take a rest. We chose some hummocks to sit on, leaving our packs on our backs. After a quick break, we headed back out. Soon after, we came across a good-sized pond.

On the far side of this pond, there was a large beaver lodge. It was about twenty feet high and sixty feet across. It must have been of prehistoric origin; I have never seen a beaver house this big. There were two giant beaver standing nearby. I made a mental note to myself to come back and trap these beavers. That is, if I found a place out here to live.

Moving on, we were getting hot and sweaty. At least we were making good headway. All of a sudden, Dan told me to stop, so I stopped.

"Walk forward, okay, stop. Dad, you're about fifteen feet downwind of me, wouldn't you say?"

"Yes, I guess the breeze is blowing from you to me. Why?"

"Well, Dad, I can still smell you."

"Okay, Dan, the next creek we come across, we will take a bath." We stunk something awful bad.

A short distance later, we encountered a very large creek, running fast and full. It wasn't deep, but it was full enough to suit our needs. Rays from the sun filtered through the leaves, sparkling off the water ripples caused by the fast-moving current. It was beautiful, a magical place all to ourselves.

We waded across the creek, removed our packs, and broke out the bars of soap. We headed to the center of this thirty-foot wide creek.

First, we washed our clothes while they were still on our bodies. We removed them, rinsed them out, and hung them up. Tree limbs hung over us, giving us shade and a place to hang our wet clothes. As we continued to wash our bodies, I heard Dan say, "Oops!"

He had dropped his soap. It was caught by the fast-moving water and was quickly swept out of sight. Without a word, I handed him another. Dan did not have to be told anything. The look in my eye was enough for him to understand not to lose the soap I handed him.

I was thinking to myself, *I better not lose my soap*, as I continued to wash my underpants. I adjusted my grip on my soap so that it wouldn't slip away, but I lost my grip on my undies. I watched the creek carry them rapidly away.

Dan laughed. "I wonder what bear is eating my bar of soap and wearing your underwear."

Since we had to wait for our clothes to dry, we took advantage of this break to get some much needed playtime in. It was the perfect place to stop for a rest. The creek had a sandy gravel bottom, and the water was not too cold. Dan climbed up onto the bank and jumped off into a deeper hole. In doing so, he bumped my glasses into the deep water. I was devastated. I knew they would be swept away, forever lost. I needed my glasses, not only to be able to see clearly, but to protect my paralyzed eye.

Dan dove in after them, even though I knew it was pointless. Not so. Dan popped up out of the water, holding his fist up high, with my glasses in his hand. He had a great big smile on his face, and he told me he was really surprised to find them. Dan's miraculous rescue saved the day.

As Dan was splashing and jumping around, he noticed something. "Dad, watch this!"

"What?" I said.

"Look at my feet when I hit the bottom. The gravel moves, and yellow stuff floats up in the water."

Sun rays peaked through the branches of the trees, and when Dan jumped down onto the gravel floor of the creek, for a moment, a yellow-colored plume floated up and danced in the sunlight, before settling back to the bottom.

I plotted this part of the creek on the map, as I had the other landmarks we had encountered on our trip.

We decided this creek was a great place to camp for the night. It was the most refreshingly rewarding of all the creeks on our hike. This was a magical place full of beautiful wonders. The creek had iron pyrite mixed with the gravel, better known as fool's gold. It also had smaller flecks of gold, known as gold flour, giving it the yellow color when the bottom was disturbed by our feet. I decided to name this creek Color Creek.

CHAPTER FIFTEEN: DAY 14

July 17, 1985

Sometime during the night, while we were fast asleep, I awoke to a very loud swooshing sound; something was disturbing the air. My head was near the screened door, so I looked out, and there was a roaring campfire. "Dan! Wake up! We have a fire on our hands."

It was our campfire from the night before. I had banked the coals before we headed to bed. I didn't completely put the fire out cold because I knew we would be using it come morning.

This was a thick muskeg root–based campfire pit; there was no soil, only living roots and mosses. The high winds had reignited the firepit of dried moss; their roots acted like a slow burning fuse.

I crawled out, still lying on the ground, and removed the grill. I reached for our frying pan and beat the fire down. Dan ran out with a kettle and hustled to the creek. Luckily, that water source was within a few feet of the tent. Dan made several trips to the creek, followed by pouring water on the firepit. I tore into the ground, digging at the root system, putting out the smoking roots. We made sure to wet the entire surrounding area, saturating everything completely.

"Thanks, Dan. Now the campfire is out cold." Another lesson we both learned, never go to bed without putting a campfire out cold. At least not here in Alaska. Moss roots are a smoldering fuse.

This work took us about an hour, then the fun was over, and we went back to sleep. Only now, I was sleeping lighter.

Morning came; another day was at hand. It seemed only a short time ago that we prevented a forest fire. After breakfast, the fire was once again put out cold. We headed off on our way. This time, we were headed to site choice number 2.

If not for this water nearby, we may have had a disastrous wildfire

There was not much for moss or tangled underbrush in this area. It had been burned off a long time ago, when a fire had swept through here. The fire had happened so long ago that the trees that had fallen had rotted away. This location looked like it had potential for good trapping someday; it would have been easy to make trails through here.

We had one last creek to cross before we reached site number 2. This creek was a long one, which began at Wien Lake, and ran out into the Muddy River. The Muddy River was several miles to our south. We crossed this creek with no problems.

There was a fair amount of trees growing here that could be used as both house logs and lumber logs. Lumber logs range from two feet in diameter to four feet in diameter. These sizes of logs are too big to be used for a house. Logs that range from fifteen inches in diameter to two feet in diameter are ideal for using to build a house.

The creek had saved the surrounding timber from succumbing to the fire that had raged through here. It also provided good drainage, which meant white spruce was abundant, instead of the stubby, stunted black spruce. White spruce is a good wood to use for construction.

Having crossed the creek, we made our way to the western base of the last hill. We walked on the second choice of land that I had picked. Between the creek we last crossed, to the base of the hill, was a mix of tamarack pine, spindly stunted black spruce, willows, and alders.

Tamarack is the only pine tree that sheds it leaves (also called needles) in the fall. A tamarack tree looks dead without its leaves. Tamarack tree fossils tell us that this breed of tree has been on earth a long time, along with two different types of ferns. When tamarack tree fossils are discovered, they always have their leaves still attached. This is evidence that they thrived in a warm climate when the trees were buried.

After we left the lower land, we enter a birch forest growing above the base of the hill. Walking up this hill with a gradual incline, seeing the plentiful supply of white birch, filled me with joy. In Alaska, we have black, white, yellow, paper, and alder trees, all of which belong to the birch family.

Would this be the piece of land that spoke to me?

I explored this hillside from top to bottom. It was facing west, which appealed to me. I made sure to thoroughly scout this area of land, opening my heart, waiting to hear if this land would speak to me. After I had physically navigated it, I knew it was not all that good of a choice.

The good points it had were the following: it had a good amount of mixed timber of size, no wildfires had been here for over three hundred years, it was an old clean forest, the trees were not close together, a fire could be controlled if done carefully, it could be cleared of rotting fuels, and this forest could stand another three hundred years, but that was about it. It did not meet my expectations, and besides, the land did not speak to me.

Near the top, we walked over a sixty-foot wide depression. It was very noticeable, with few trees of any size growing on the pronounced dipping ground. Walking over this area gave a hollow sounding reverberation, somewhat like that of a drum—a big drum. To me, it looked like a closed in and sagging sinkhole, with a root system cover. Most likely, it was a huge melting block of ice, covered by volcanic ash. This is a common occurrence across the Alaskan terrain. Bears are known to hibernate in these ice cave sinkholes.

There were a few other reasons why I did not find interest in this area. There was no flat ground on which to have a lawn or garden. There was no real view here, except for the western mountain range. That is not to say the range wasn't pretty. Northwestern cold winds blowing on this hill face would make for cold winters. The nearest source for water was the creek, nearly two miles away. Also, there was a forest of trees that would need to be removed, just to have a southern view of the sun. The biggest reason for passing up this site was the lack of sunlight, other than the sunset. I wanted a place exposed to a full day of sun, not just a sunset. Nope. It did not take long to decide that this was not the land I wanted.

Without further delay, we set our compass for the third and final choice, located on the southern face of this hill. We still had the large photo to refer to for other targets, should the third place prove to be a bust. I had very thoroughly gone over the map for a full year before I had narrowed down to these three choices. I was confident one of my choices would be fitting for my dreams.

Starting near the top of the hill we were on, we headed eastward, following at the same elevation. We crossed several narrow ridges and ravines. The south face of this hill we were leaving was heavily forested. There was a mix of different types of birch trees, spruces, and a few different cottonwoods. There was no shortage of firewood here.

We entered an area that had a wildfire burn through in the past. The burned area came from the north and ended on the southern face of the hill, which we were traveling from. The wildfire had been extensive toward the north. The burned area had recovered well, with new young growth. There were many standing trees, which had been killed by the fire. All of the dead, yet standing trees, would make good firewood for heating a house. There was enough to last for years to come, as long as it could be harvested before the wood rotted. This potential use of the burn was in my mind's eye.

The aftermath of a wildfire is not pretty, but it is nature's way (when it occurs without man's intervention). This crossing was slow because of the mix of deadwood and new growth. Much like we had experienced earlier on our trip.

Only you can prevent forest fires.

Crossing this burned landscape was not fun, and it was dangerous. We had to be diligently careful. We were so close to my third site, it was hard to control the urge to plunge onward. The day was getting long; we were tired. We could easily make mistakes in this state of weariness, mistakes that we couldn't afford. We had to maintain a methodical pace to ensure our safety. Being deliberately diligent can be a wee bit frustrating, especially when the end of our race was so near.

"Look for a space for the tent, Dan." An unreasonable amount of time had passed, and still we had not found a good place to camp. This campground (pun intended) had no openings in the trees for a tent to be set up. If I had not lost my hand axe, it would be a simple matter of chopping down some trees. I had my hunting knife and the machete, but the trees here were too large for these tools to tackle.

Using those tools would be time-consuming, so it seemed easier to find an open area. We finally stumbled on a place that was big enough for a tent. There was just one problem; it had a tree right in the center. "Dan! You need to test fire that shotgun on the base of that tree."

"That's a big 10-4, Dad."

Blam!

We watched the tree fall, pitched our tent, and called it a day. "Thank you, God." Or should I have said "guardian angel?"

CHAPTER SIXTEEN: DAY 15

July 18, 1985

t was another morning that we were low on water. After breakfast, I told Dan to stay at camp while I went ahead to find and bring back water, marking my trail as I went. Marking trail required a different method this time. The young, short trees were easy to snap at waist height. This helped make a clear trail for our packs to travel through, and was easy to follow.

To my surprise, I was soon out of the burn area. An old forest of very large trees appeared. It looked so good, in fact, that I turned around and headed back to get Dan.

"Boy, Dad! That was a quick trip!"

"I broke out of this entangled mess, Dan. We will pack up and push on. There should be no problem in finding water."

We came to the old forest of big trees, larger than any we had seen during the whole trip. Here was the first large birch I had seen during our trek. We had seen many large white spruces, but not any large birch. Many birch here were all of three feet in diameter, and healthy.

As we traveled deeper into this forest, I began to see a spectacular view. There was plenty of sun above the forest canopy. Also, it was facing the south, meaning we would have sun even during the shortest days of the year.

I was begging to have an emotional connection to the land. There was large birch, large white spruce, and a big area on which to have a garden, lawn, and greenhouse. There was a two-hundred-foot drop-off on this land, with a picture-perfect view. The soil was excellent with no permafrost and good drainage. I would have to remove some trees, but I could see the possibilities for a future here. I could foresee the potential of what I could do with this land.

Ever since we had come into the old growth forest, we had been traveling in a single file line. Dan was using his knife, re-blazing the birch above my ax blazing, by peeling a one-inch wide portion of the outer bark. In the removal of only the outermost bark of a birch tree, a black ring of the exposed wood is left behind. I blazed on both sides of our trail, slashing in deep to the heartwood (the wood under the layer of the innermost bark), marking where we came from and the way we were headed. Blazing like this, we could backtrack if need be. It was a unique marking system.

Traveling east onto this third choice, we came up to a good-sized ridgeline. This ridge line ran north to south. I found a sizable, well used animal game trail up on this ridge. Migrating caribou had established this well used trail, and now all the local animals were using it.

It was easy to see why the caribou and other animals used this ridge as a pathway. It was naturally formed, as though it was meant to be used as an animal highway. We went over this ridge and on down to the valley in search of water. We found a flowing spring coming out of the gravelly ground, right at the base of this hill. We filled up on the natural spring water, marveling in all the wonders. And to think with all the resources this area had to offer, yet it was my third choice.

I wanted to explore some more, so we turned back and followed the ridge to the top. Once we reached the top, we examined the layout of the ground. It was a part of the forest that had flourished since the burn had ripped through here. Mind you, all of this land was covered with trees, but I could see a strip of land that could someday be an airstrip.

It was like I was dancing on air while we followed this trail on back down to where we had first reached the ridge. We made our way over to the drop away point on this ridge and peered out over the valley. We could see the five lakes, located nearly six hundred feet lower than where we stood.

We could also see Mount Roosevelt, the mountain we had flown over on our trip to Lake Minchumina. Beyond Roosevelt, we could see the Alaska Mountain Range, majestic in her beauty, running for some seventy-seven miles. The most impressive and powerful of all Mother Nature's creations in our view was Denali Mountain—all 20,320 feet of the glorious beauty.

I heard the voice of this land speaking to me, "Choose me."

Denali in all its splendorous glory

The day was shining brilliantly. Not a cloud could be found marring the blue heavens above, as we stood looking over the vast Alaskan wilderness.

Denali Mountain!

Denali was at the cusp of our southern view, appearing as though it was balanced at the edge of the earth.

"Dan, this is where I will build my log home."

"Here, Dad?"

"Yes, right here. On this very spot we are standing."

For a long moment, I stood looking over the panorama. My mind was working like a newsroom—computing, compiling, analyzing. The paper of plans was ready to print, as a tingling came rushing over me. The hair on the back of my neck stood up. Dan was looking out over this vast, wonderful view with me.

"Just like a picture, Dad."

"Yup, this will be where the front window will be with a deck. Drive that claim stake in."

Our journey was complete; my dreams were answered. Our fifty-seven-mile hike had all been worth it.

"This is it."

Dan and I seeing my future in the Alaskan wilderness

"I set the compass bearing headed for that large lake, the one where we saw the twenty-foot lodge on its northwestern shore. We will pay those settlers a visit. From there, we will hop a flight back to Fairbanks."

"Let's go!"

We headed back down to where the flowing spring was located, about four hundred feet from the place I had decided I would build my house. Once again, we filled our canteens. "With any luck, Dan, we will be visiting our new neighbors tonight."

The spring led to well-trimmed willow thickets. The moose had been dining on the willows, like cows grazing in a pasture. The willows were maintained at shoulder height, with an abundance of moose tracks and trails leading through them. I felt as though I had found my own Garden of Eden.

We followed through the willows, but traveling was slow. We couldn't see any landmarks, so I relied mainly on the compass to keep the right course. Occasional obstacles had to be skirted, but we followed a straight path for the most part.

Suddenly, we snapped to attention, hearing a loud *thump! Thump! Crash! Smash! Crashing!*

"Wow!"

We were facing our first close moose encounter of our entire journey. We must have been walking right toward that bull moose, otherwise he would have let us walk on by. This moose had been lying low, hiding motionlessly until we came too close for comfort, and he jumped up running away. This is normal moose behavior, but it sure was funny seeing a huge moose with a seven-foot rack plowing a path like a bulldozer through the trees and bushes.

"See where he went, Dan? He went the same way we are headed; he has made a trail for us."

"The guarding angel is still with us, Dad."

Bullwinkle knew where to go alright; he dozed on out of the heavy thickets and onto a more open area. He headed toward a place where there was a creek and larger trees.

Dan was behind me while I was doing my best to follow the compass heading. All of a sudden, Dan firmly shouted with the utmost commanding voice, "Dad! Walk fast for a hundred feet. Stop and rest."

Without hesitation, I did as he ordered. (We had a rule: any direct orders were to be acted upon without hesitation.) After I had gone about a hundred feet, I found a log and sat on it.

I looked back at Dan. He was making a wide arc around the path I had just taken. He came and sat next to me.

"Well? Tell me what I did that for!"

"I was following behind, and I saw you step on wet newspaper. Or so it looked, until I saw the bees swarming from the surrounding ground. Those bees were looking for you, Dad. As soon as I saw them, I had you get clear right quick!"

"Thanks, Dan, I owe you another one."

Continuing on, we walked along a small creek that led us to a hidden, creepy lagoon. The area was covered by overhanging trees, camouflaging an active beaver pond. They went on about their work, paying no attention to us as we watched them. Three beavers were busily chewing the base of a cottonwood. Then like lumberjacks, they watched it as it fell. Two were on the wrong side and moved out of the way. This tree fell partway, and then hung up on another tree.

I decided to name the beaver Larry, Moe, and Curly since that is what they reminded me of. Each looked as though they were blaming the others for this tree getting hung up. They wasted little time arguing before they moved on to the smaller tree that had hung up their prize. I tell you, their teeth slice chips out of a green tree like a lumberjack swinging an ax. Before the first chip hit the ground, a second one was in the air.

Two beavers worked on this tree, as the third one stood supervising, as though he was the boss. It wasn't long before both trees were down, and the three of them moved away. They took no time to celebrate or shake paws. Rather, they immediately began snipping the limbs off the trees and dragged them into the pond.

"Shows over, Dan. Now we know where the term 'busy as a beaver' comes from." We left the beavers to their work and continued on our hike.

We entered an open area covered with tall bear grass. (In the lower forty-eight states, this grass is called slough grass.) I was looking ahead, knocking down the tall grass in front of me, while Dan followed behind on my trail.

Something caught my eye that put me on full alert. "Geesh!" I gasped, as I swung my bear gun around to focus my aim. All of this happened in the blink of an eye.

I held my fire and took a closer look at what it was. It was a fifty-five gallon rusty brown barrel. It looked just like a brown bear out of the corner of my eye. This was bear grass after all, and this grass did not get its name for nothing. "Dad, you sure moved that shotgun fast. What the heck is a rusty barrel doing in the middle of nowhere?"

The barrel had been punctured on both ends using a fire ax, and the part resting on the marshy ground had rusted away.

"Dan, this barrel has been here for years, perhaps since World War II or later. Maybe it was left behind during the cleanup of the old fuel drum depot, at Lake Minchumina. I'm only guessing, of course. I suspect the small tundra ponds in this area were dumping grounds in those times. The air-dropped empty fuel drums, would sink and rust, disappearing for ever more. Mother Nature does the cleansing. The drums were air-dropped from a big plane like bombs, but first they were fire axed on both ends, in order for them to sink fast. There are likely more in this area, but most would have been dropped in the deeper ponds. This one may have been dropped during the winter months, when this area would have been all covered with snow, and probably appeared to the pilot as a tundra pond."

This grassy area was a bit tricky to traverse because it was a boggy, grass-covered, matted marsh.

"Don't follow close, Dan, and step easy. It wouldn't take much to poke through into water. Tread lightly. We may have to change our path if it gets more dangerous."

The grass bobbed up and down with each step we took. Even the small black trees were swaying to and fro. It was like we were walking on water with pontoons on.

"We have to keep an eye on each other, Dan. Get that rope out, and keep it in a handy place."

One by one, we made our way from small tree to small tree, searching for firmer footing. It was an eerie feeling to see the trees moving and wobbling about.

I recalled seeing this area when I was scouting earlier, from the spot I staked my claim. There was a wooded area on the other side of this floating ground; we only had to make it there to have stable footing. Beyond the wooded area was where the lake should have been, but since we could not see over the trees here, I wasn't totally confident in its location.

We finally reached firm ground. The floating grass was, thankfully, part of our past. It was a good feeling to be back on solid ground, where the trees didn't wobble. I get motion sickness fairly easy, but I was far more concerned with one of us falling through, than of me getting sick.

After traveling some distance in this forest, I felt as though we should have arrived at the lake. It was getting late in the afternoon. The absence of waterfowl noises indicated to me that we were far from any lake. "Dan, it is time to climb a tree!"

"These trees don't have any limbs to help me climb, Dad."

"*Okay, Dan.* It's my turn to climb a tree. We need to find that lake." I took off my pack and shinnied up. Crossing my legs, hugging the tree, I worked my way up this skinny tree. I could see two lakes. One was hard to our right, and the other was hard to the left of the direction we were heading.

"*Okay, Dan!*"

"Well, which way, Dad?"

"That way. I'll set the compass for that direction so we stay on track."

I climbed down and told Dan, "We are in between two lakes. If we continue on in the same direction, we would have hit the third lake some time tomorrow, but we would have missed our intended lake."

"How did you do it, Dad?"

"Do what?"

"Climb that tree?"

I explained to Dan the method I had used, and since he had watched me climb, he should have no problem shinning up the tree in the same manner. "I have to try that, Dad." Dan had no problem and could now put one more skill under his belt.

It was 2:00 a.m. when we reached the lake. We saw beavers swimming, ducks, seagulls, and, best of all, two cabins. One was straight across from us. It was the same one we had saw from the hill several days before. The other was to our right, and far away. We had not been able to see this cabin until now. Only the hard-working beavers were awake. One was swimming close by us, pulling a tree branch. Dan wanted to shoot the beaver for fresh meat. "Dan, we would wake the people here. This is not the right time."

CHAPTER SEVENTEEN: DAY 16

July 19, 1985

We set up camp shortly after 2:00 a.m. in this morning. Yesterday had been a long day. The sun was shining brightly when we woke up, and there was a slight wind, making the lake a little choppy. Any more wind and it would have had whitecaps. When we had arrived the night before, the lake had been smooth as glass. The wind was a blessing; it helped blow away the pesky mosquitoes.

We made pancakes for breakfast, the kind of mix that only needed water. Pancakes proved to last us a long time on this trip and made for hearty meals. This lake was round and lined with a mix of trees. On down to our right is where the lake's outlet is at. To the south, there was a small hill, approximately forty feet high. Looking a quarter mile northward from the outlet, there was a cabin. This home sat back from the shore about three hundred feet. Swinging more to the left, I could see no signs of other people. I continued searching the terrain and saw straight across from us a pretty sight.

A cabin was set on a hill, which was about twenty feet above the waterline and set back about a hundred feet. There was nothing else on the lake that I could see; for sure there weren't any air-o-planes. According to the list of claims on the map I had, there should be at least six dwelling sites on this lake.

I needed the map of sites claimed to ensure I didn't stake on land that was already taken. Once a piece of land was claimed, whether the person proved up on the land to qualify for a patent or not, it was no longer available. The Bureau of Land Management would not allow it, even if the person who had claimed the land was never going to return.

"Look, Dan, over near the shore at that cabin. It's the dwelling we thought was a twenty-foot lodge. What is that, Dan?"

"Looks like a yellow raft with two people, Dad!"

"I see now. They're flying a kite. Well I'll be darned!" The only place with room enough to fly a kite in this area is on the lake.

"Okay, Dan. Let's get their attention. Hand me the signal mirror." I angled the mirror so the sun rays would reflect back in the direction of the canoe. It had no effect. Apparently, they couldn't see our flashing light because they were too busy looking up at the kite.

"Dan, it's time to use the cannon (shotgun). This ought a get their attention."

Being careful to make sure the gun was pointed at a safe impact area, I fired. *Boom!* The bang of the gunshot echoed back and forth through the region. All this time, Dan, continued using the signal mirror. "Looks like we have been seen. They're reeling in the kite."

Dan said an enthusiastic, "*Yes!*" The canoe headed back to shore, and its passengers went up to the cabin. Rather than packing up the tent, we waited for whatever would happen next.

One of the people came back to the raft and began to paddle toward us. Mind you, on our side of the lake, the water was rough with white caps. The lake was round and was a mile wide. Crossing this lake with a raft was not a speedy process. The man in his raft was slowly making his way toward us. It was not a very large rubber raft and didn't appear to be of high quality. *I hope he knows what he is doing*, I thought to myself. When he was within hailing distance, I called out, "*Ahoy in the raft!*"

"You okay?"

"Yes!" Dan and I both said at once.

While he was still paddling toward us, introductions took place. His name was Mark Weronko. His four-year-old son, Toby, and he were flying the kite. Mark had taken his son back to the cabin, grabbed a first aid kit, and came to us.

"Why the first aid kit?" I asked.

"I thought you came down in a plane crash. How did you get here?"

"We walked in from Lake Minchumina."

Mark's immediate reply was "Walked? Nobody walks in. Everyone flies in."

Mark pulled his raft ashore, and we shook hands. A long visit ensued. Mark was a talker and was full of questions. He suggested we leave our packs, tent, and gear to come back for it tomorrow. "This is only a three-man raft," he explained, "and you know how that is always overrated."

"I know." Pointing to our tent, I said, "That is rated for four." We all shared a laugh.

This was a three-man raft, and we proved it. It was also a wet trip, a real balancing act. The raft could have used more air. The water was constantly lapping in on us, as we spread apart the best we could.

Mark was a talkative, friendly fellow. He talked the whole way across the lake. It was no wonder why Mark was talkative. His wife, Katie, his son, Toby, and himself had been out here for all of ninety days, with no one else to talk to. Mark only had the one paddle; otherwise, I would have helped. Heading into the wind was interesting; every time he stopped paddling, we drifted back a ways. Nearing the shelter on the lee side of the lake, we started gaining more headway.

The shore was abrupt; there was no sandbar or weeds. The water came right up to the tree line of leaning black spruce, with a small space of bank. From there, we went on up through the trees on a well-made path. It felt good to step out onto solid ground, after that wet, bobbing raft trip.

Mark led the way up to his cabin and introduced his wife, Katie, and their four-year-old son, Toby. We told them our names and explained again that we had walked in from Lake Minchumina.

These words, which I will never forget as long as I live, came from Toby Weronko: "*Ya krazy!*"

My immediate reply was "You got that right!" We all had a laugh at that. If there was any ice between them and us, it evaporated instantly.

Katie was a nice lady; she made us feel right at home. She didn't have to talk much; Mark was doing that. He shared with us their whole story, and then showed us around their place.

The cabin they had been working on was built on top of stilts. The stilts were made out of wood posts, which had been dug down to the hard permafrost ground. The cabin had to be well vented. This was accomplished by building the cabin high above the ground, to keep the frozen permafrost from thawing, or the cabin would sink. The cabin was in the construction stage, but it was closed in and had a roof. It also had a window and one door. Porch stringers were there, but the deck wasn't built yet. The cabin was sixteen feet long and twelve feet wide. It had a ceiling over eight feet high, with a trapdoor in the floor, where items were stored.

The roof was a half pitch, constructed of plywood covered by pieces of cut plywood. These pieces of plywood had to fit in a small plane, so they were only four feet by two feet in size. Topping his roof, Mark used materials that no one will see used in this fashion again. Mark had used tin to top his roof, for its waterproof properties, but it was a special tin.

During this time period, the '80s, printer's plates were used for the printing of newspapers. Printing plates are light gauge metal sheets, the size of a double page of a newspaper. The print was on one side, and other side was blank. They would be used once, for the day's newspaper, before being sent back and melted down. Then the process would start all over again.

Somehow, Mark managed to buy some of these printing sheets off the *News-Miner*. The *News-Miner* was the newspaper company in Fairbanks. Mark only had to pay two cents per sheet. The plates are as light as paper and made of aluminum. They are shiny on one side and dark on the other. The dark side is where the words were printed. Mark used a staple gun to shingle his roof out of these printer's plates. They were not thick or hard, but they did the job.

Mark was a frugal person. He did all the shopping and made sure to find deals on everything. When he shopped at grocery stores, he asked the managers for the items that would soon be tossed and was given them for a lesser price.

Another item Mark would buy at half price was damaged canned goods. He would buy them by the case. These cans only had aesthetic damage, such as dents or missing labels. He developed a pretty good idea of each can's contents that had missing labels, after years of securing food this way.

Bakery goods that were past their sell by date, were often free, or in some marginal cases, half price. When Mark would stay in town on his own, he knew the places he could get free meals and cheap overnight places to sleep.

Mark made good money. He worked for Northwest Airlines, in Anchorage, Alaska. He worked as a tractor driver, towing the big passenger planes in and around the airports. He could even get the planes in and out of hangars, a very responsible job.

The cabin had no furniture, only a few necessities. There was a portable gasoline stove that needed to be hand-pumped to pressurize it, a camp gasoline pressure pump stove, a small one-room cast-iron airtight wood stove for heat. For seating, they simply sat on their stacks and stacks of cases of canned foods. They had buckets and wash tubs for washing. There were no cupboards, just a box for their cooking ware. Mind you, they we only getting set up. They had done well, considering the time they had been at it and what resources they had.

They had put a lot of hard work into building the cabin. Some of the logs had been dragged in by hand, from nearby woods. Many had been floated on the lake and brought up from their beach. Mark had no experience in building a log cabin, but he had been a genius in the way he did the log walls.

He would round notch the overlapping corners in a typical fashion. Then using his chainsaw, he would ripsaw in between the new log placed, and that last log placed. He would run the chainsaw through the space between two logs a few times, until the flattened wood was a snug fit. While his way of laying up a big wall was effective, by no means would I recommend it be copied or encouraged. It was a tedious, diligent work of art.

Floor joists were made of flat-sided logs. Beneath the floor he had 10" fiberglass insulation, with metal 1/4" screen to hold and protect the insulation.

Mark informed us that they were waiting for a pilot friend of theirs living in Fairbanks. The pilot was overdue in coming out to pick up Katie and Toby for some shopping and medical checkups. The plane should be dropping in any day now. He went on to tell us, as far as he could tell, no one else was out here on any of the lakes right now. There was a bunch of people that had claimed land the first day the settlement area was open for claiming, but most left and would never come back.

There were other settlers who had not started to prove up, but still had time to. He said he was not a military veteran and, therefore, had to live in a proven habitable dwelling for five months each year, for five consecutive years. Mark's claim had not yet been inspected, to prove he had built a habitable dwelling. Only after the inspection was done would the BLM start counting his time living out here. Katie and Toby would be the primary residents while Mark would go between working in Fairbanks and living out here. "Katie is not too keen on the idea of being out here by herself. It will be hard to prove up in the time I am allotted."

CHAPTER EIGHTEEN: DAY 17

July 20, 1985

We slept upstairs in their cabin the previous night while Mark, Katie, and Toby slept in the room below. After breakfast, Mark filled the raft full of air so that it could carry all of our stuff in one trip. Fortunately, the lake was as smooth as glass for this journey.

I was relieved to see that no bear had come by to destroy our belongings. After all, our stuff sat there most of a day, and all of the night. It was an incessant worry of mine.

"That guardian angel, Dan, was looking after it."

When we were done retrieving our things, and had left them at Mark's cabin, he took us around the lake to show us the other structures. All of the structures had been long ago abandoned, although Mark shared each and every one of their stories with us.

Exploring the lake and the remnants of others'
attempt to make a life on a homestead

On our way to the one at the south end of the lake, we paddled
by a bull moose, who paid us no attention. It seemed as though he
knew Mark's yellow raft and was not in the least worried of him. I
snapped a few photos.

He took us by one of the cabins and explained that it belonged
to a young couple, the Carries. Mr. Carrie had intended to stake a
claim on land far up the hill from the lake. After trudging through
the tangled mess of undergrowth for some distance, carrying a pack
and a five-gallon bucket, he changed his mind. He had only made it
halfway up the hill. He returned to the shore and said, "This will be
better."

The couple went about building a crude cabin, made of trees
that were more suitable in size to be used for fence posts. They lived
in a tent at first, like everyone did. By winter, they had moved in.
They hadn't bothered with peeling any of the logs they used to
construct the house, and there were gaps of space between their walls
all over. They had attempted to keep warm by stuffing anything they
could find into these cracks. They used paper, fiberglass, and rags,
but mostly they used cardboard tacked up on the walls.

This stopped the breezes, but it didn't keep out the cold. The
small wood heating stove was by far not enough to keep them warm.
Their intentions were good. They had built a cold entry with a door
and a door to the inner room. They had a medium-sized generator

and lots of gasoline. They had made a bed that hung from the ceiling and could swing. It was the size of a double bed but had no mattress. Instead, they had used moss they dug up for comfort.

Hundreds of gallons of gasoline were used to keep them warm while they were under their electric blanket in bed. I expect that was a lot of the time. Mark told me more, but I could fill another book if I wrote it all down. In time, they gave it up. It was not for the lack of trying; they gave it their all. They were flown out, back to civilization. There are many dreams people have throughout life that get dashed out. Their dream, sadly, ended as well.

The saddest story of the failed homesteaders belonged to a house that was just past Mark's place, on the north end of the lake. The Weeks: father, mother, daughter, and daughter's boyfriend. All they had managed to construct in their attempt to build a home was the posts for the foundation. They had an octagon-shaped base, made from big spruce logs. Clearly, they were planning on building a large home. A few things went deeply wrong with their plans.

This could have been a magnificent home

The first problem the Weeks encountered was making a deal with a pilot. The deal was the Weeks would make an airstrip out here, and in exchange, the pilot would fly out deliveries of supplies for them. This sounded like it would have been a good deal.

They had planned to have a guide business, where interested parties would be flown in by this pilot. This way, they could make money guiding people on moose hunts and other similar activities.

They cleared all the trees, filled in the low spots with timber beams, and cleared the brush. They were making good progress, as they put most of their time into accomplishing this. All this time, they lived in a ten-man tent. The pilot never came back, leaving them high and dry.

The second problem they encountered happened because no plane ever came out, and they ran out of food. During this time period, there were others living on this lake, as well as two residents on the nearest neighboring lake. The father and boyfriend were forced to hunt, in order to supply food for the family.

The father killed a bear, and it was too much meat to keep in the summer, so they held a block party. In this case, it was a two-lake party. Well, you can probably guess what happened next. The remains attracted more bear, and that meant more kills were done, and more two-lake parties. All this time, they were still thinking a plane was going to come in.

The third problem they were faced with was running out of mosquito repellent. To keep the mosquitoes at bay, they had smudge fires to make smoke, helping to keep the bloodsucking bugs at bay. Still, no plane had arrived, and fall was coming on. The boyfriend agreed to make a hike to Wien Lake, some twelve miles north of their camp, to see if they could find any help. On Wien Lake, there was a lodge, and in those days, the only way of communications way out there was a ham radio, but nobody had one of those.

The young man made it to Wien Lake, after two days of travel. A plane came back, and soon after, the entire family left for parts unknown. I heard later that one of the people who had been living out on one of these lakes reported the father for shooting bear out of season, and the father was fined. To me, it made no sense to fine a man whose family was facing starvation, and he provided food the only way that he could. Like a game warden had once told me, "It's not me who you need to be worried about. It's your neighbors."

Back at Mark's place, we set up our tent behind their cabin. One food item that Mark had a surplus of was Spam. He had every kind of Spam you can imagine. Katie was good at making it in several different ways. Katie would make Spam sandwiches, Spam burgers, biscuits with a slice of Spam and a slice of cheese, and several other recipes that were tasty.

That night, Mark and Katie told us of Bernard Prudeau, a resident who had been on the neighboring lake. Bernard had been there for six months. He built a cabin and then went back to his home in France. Not being an American citizen, he was not eligible to stake land. He wanted to have the experience, so he found a person in Wasilla, Alaska, that had staked a claim.

The American had given permission to Bernard to build a cabin on his claim. This land claimer had staked in 1982, on opening day. He was one of several people who staked a claim and never came back, or had the time to prove up.

When Bernard saw this attempted homesteader's name on the filling map, he looked him up and asked him if he could build a cabin on his land. He would build it at no expense, using the material on site. Then all this man had to do was live there and finish his prove up, to meet whatever his requirements were. The building would be completed within the time allotted. In any case, Bernard only wanted the experience.

The Weronkos were impressed with Bernard and his work ethics. They admired his preparedness, skills, and his attitude on life. The Weronkos and the Frenchman had exchanged visits from time to time, by walking to and from each other's campsites. Toby, at his early age of four, walked the entire way there and back, quite a feat for such a little guy.

Bernard, all of five feet tall, was dropped off by the man who did the staking with his simple hand tools, a bed roll, clothes, and several five-gallon buckets of dry pinto beans. A date was set for Bernard to be picked up six months later, before the lake froze over at the end of September, in 1984. April to the end of September were good months to get his work accomplished. Mark told us we had to see what Bernard had built. On my topographic map, he marked the way to walk to his place.

CHAPTER NINETEEN: DAY 18

July 21, 1985

This morning, we set out bright and early for Bernard's cabin. We wanted to make sure we were back in time for Katie's Spam burgers.

On our walk over there, we traveled around the lake. We followed as close to the shore line as we could, taking the moose paths. At some point, Dan commented, "I can't believe that Toby made this walk. He is one tough kid."

"That he is, Dan, like you are. Only he is a lot younger. Toby knows firsthand what it's like walking in this jungle. That's why his first words to us after being told we had walked in from Lake Minchumina were '*Ya krazy!*'"

We reached the grassy shore of the lake where Bernard had built a cabin. We found the trail marked, just as Mark had told us. The trail was about 1/4 mile back into the taller timber, away from the scrub spruce. This path had been well used by the Frenchman. We came upon a clearing set in the woods and discovered a small, gypsy-rounded style of cabin. It looked like a cabin found in children's storybooks, but this one was real. I was already impressed from the first sight. It looked inviting, and yet lonely, like it had been waiting for company.

I said, "Hello Frenchman's Cabin. I have heard a lot about you."

It was built on a low mound, with a slight rise above the ground level. It was low in height, had a flat roof, was small in size, and had a big double pane window at the end of the cabin we first saw, with wood peeled bars to keep the bear from smashing it. On the back side, we found a small door made of draw knifed poles tightly fitted, with metal hinges for the door to open outward. The handle was of a natural curved wood. It only had an outside latch; the door had a snug, airtight fit and was up off the ground, on a pole-flattened floor, fitted tight. When I opened the door, it was like pulling open a vault door sealed tight, with no air leaks, whatsoever.

This cabin was made from fine craftsmanship

Dan standing in front of the Frenchman's Cabin

This world-traveling Frenchman, Bernard Prudeau, had managed to build this incredible structure with just a few minor tools, a handful of supplies, and the necessities for sustaining his life while he built it. The Frenchman, for his quality work, gets an A+ grade from me.

CHAPTER TWENTY

Our Alaskan Wilderness Adventure Ends

We woke up early and shared a pancake breakfast with the Weronko family. We had given what was left of our traveling food to Katie. For the next several days, we helped Mark with projects that he needed to get done. We wanted to help make up for all that this family had given us, during our extended stay. Our plane was days overdue, so there was no better way to spend the time than helping our future neighbors. We cut, split, and stacked firewood, built a food cache that also served as an observation tower, and began digging a root cellar.

While digging the root cellar, I discovered that the ground under Mark's home was part of a natural ridge, probably formed by a fold in the earth's crust millions of years ago. The rock in this area consisted of red and black sandstone. The sandstone had been covered by trees and mosses, so I had not noticed it before. The ridgeline was fractured and tilted, running around the lake's shoreline.

Finding this ridgeline made it clear to me why the lake was rounded, with higher banks on two sides of the lake while its center was twenty-five feet deep. This was not a normal, shallow tundra pond with grasses, but a basin of oil-bearing sandstone, with very little grass.

I found this very intriguing. I became a tunnel rat and started busting sandstone with the tools I had available. I used fire to fracture the sandstone, with the intent to make a unique stone cellar out of nature's resources. I made it to be a self-supporting structure. I asked Mark about what he had found while digging the post holes for the cabin.

"This frozen sand," he said.

"It might be frozen, but it will never sink. Your cabin is on sandstone."

I took photos of the setting sun from the Weronkos' cabin while Dan and Mark were in front of the cabin. This photo, along with others that Dan and I had taken on our journey, I will cherish forever. The photo of the sun setting near the Weronkos' cabin has been enlarged and hangs in a few of my friends' homes.

The Weronkos and their unfinished cabin

One morning, I had some sort of medical malady affecting my torso. The pain was like no other pain I had ever had before. It was so bad, I thought that I might be dying. This pain started low in my back and steadily became worse. I tried rolling on the ground in the hopes of finding a comfortable position for the pain to go away, but nothing worked. The pain got worse.

Mark had a medical book. He was busy looking up all the symptoms that I could barely relate to him while being in excruciating pain. I had the attention of everyone. Dan was especially concerned. Mark, among other possible explanations, was looking for a possible poisoning. He was asking me if I had eaten any wild water plants; there was hemlock in places along the shore.

"No! I know not to eat those."

This day happened to be a Thursday, one of the allotted days for the mail to be brought out by plane. This plane came from Fairbanks, out to Lake Minchumina. It was the only regular air traffic we could expect in this remote area.

I told Dan, "Go get the red distress flares we brought, and have them ready." The flares were handheld, and when fired, they would shoot high into the sky bursting brightly.

We saw the plane far off in the distance, headed toward Lake Minchumina. Our location was set back from the plane's view. From our position, we were facing the backside of the plane.

Between my intolerable bouts of pain, and a few short words with Mark, we agreed he should shoot the flare as the plane headed back to Fairbanks. That was our best chance for the pilot to see the flare. If there was not a clear indication that the pilot had seen the flare, we would fire additional flares to get his attention.

Dan heard it first. "It's coming back!"

We could see it flying from our right, headed toward our left. It was time. Mark fired a flare. It traveled high, then burst, floating down slowly in a big ball of sparkling red light. There was an immediate response. The plane rocked side to side, the wings reflecting in the sun. They saw us!

The plane was miles away and continued to fly on. The plane was the type that had to land on its wheels; it made no sense for this pilot to try and come help us. We knew they would report the flare, its location, and the time when we fired it to the authorities.

The pain had begun around 9:00 a.m. and was becoming worse with every passing hour. I tried not to make a big fuss, such as carrying on, or even crying. I did not want to exasperate everyone's feelings even more. I was cringing enough already. I didn't want Dan to leave my side. I held his hand while he tended to my needs and suggestions. I was thinking of words to tell him if the time for me to pass should come.

I passed on supper and crawled into the tent. Dan ate while sitting by my side. It was then I asked Dan to get me a five-gallon bucket to sit on, to try to go to the bathroom to relieve myself. It seemed to be helping, sitting there. Something was passing. What, I did not know, but it felt good. (Could it have been a kidney stone?)

During the night, I found it better to lay one side in a fetal position. I had Dan use his fingertips to lightly touch my skin, moving them around my back over the area I was having the pain. It was soothing.

Finally, the pain left. This happened at 10:00 p.m. Dan went ahead and told Mark I was okay, and we all slept well the rest of the night.

State of Alaska troopers coming to the rescue

Bright and early after breakfast, an orange and white helicopter approached, noisily hovering overhead, while circling us. It was the State of Alaska troopers. They had a megaphone speaker and were saying something, but the noise was too deafening to understand what was being said. Mark rafted out to open water, to lead them to an area on the shoreline where they could land. The chopper hovered to shore, landed, and cut off the engine.

When the blades stopped, a swat officer in a blue uniform with a bulletproof vest, jumped out. He was carrying an AR-15 rifle, held at port arms. He was below us but was rapidly approaching. I turned to Dan and said, "Do not make a move, or touch a gun."

Having had experience in the army, I knew that no sudden moves should be made at this time. The trooper walked up the hill to us and stood next to our tent, behind the cabin. His rifle was pointing off to his side and upward, with his finger on the trigger guard.

The officer was only a short distance away. He asked if this was a medical emergency. I spoke up, telling him, "It was yesterday, but the severe pain I had cleared up last night."

He looked straight into our eyes, then pulled the bolt on his rifle open and grasped the bullet. He removed it and removed the magazine as well. At that moment, I felt at ease.

"Wow! You sure came loaded for bears!"

Alaska State Trooper swat officer carrying an AR-15

The trooper went on to tell us that a lesson was learned a month ago at Manly, Alaska. A trooper friend had been shot dead while in a chopper, by a man who went nuts and was killing people at will. "We stopped him, but we are more alert now."

The trooper asked us if there was anything he could do for us now. Mark said, "Yes," and handed him a phone number to call. It was the number for the Fairbanks pilot, who was overdue.

"Thank you for coming, officer."

Apparently, the flare worked, and the mail plane had called it in. The trooper loaded back into the chopper, cranked it up, and flew off back to Fairbanks.

Mark turned to me and said, "Katie and Toby should fit in the plane with you and Dan. If I went along on the same trip, there wouldn't be room for you and Dan, and I don't want you two to have to wait for a different plane."

In the early morning, a float plane came right on in, without circling. He cut his engine and drifted to shore. Before the engine had a chance to cool, we were in the air and off to Fairbanks. I paid for the flight; it was the least I could do.

After an hour and a half, the big city of Fairbanks came into view just ahead of us. I thought to myself, *I wonder if I still know how to drive*. A funny thought, I know, but thoughts like that happen when you haven't been behind a wheel for some time.

From the air looking down, we had quite a view. There were cars narrowly missing one another and people milling about. I looked for a float pond, but none were in sight. We continued getting lower and lower to the ground. I could see we were low enough that cars were driving alongside us. Finally, I felt the floats touch water. We had landed on the Chena River, in Fairbanks. The plane taxied up to the pilot's dock, and the pilot drove us to the storage lot where I had left my pickup. We had come full circle, starting and ending our Alaskan wilderness adventure at the same spot. We were ready to drive back down the Alaskan Canadian Highway to Minnesota.

The following spring of 1986, I would return and start the work of making my dream come true. A piece of heaven in the center of Alaska, a land I could call my own, a home and a future where anything was possible.

To begin the adventure of *Ose Mountain Alaska*.

To be continued.

ABOUT THE AUTHOR

Duane is new to the writing world, but not new to the world of experience. He was born and raised in Minnesota, overlooking the river valley. Duane graduated from Echo High School in 1960. He enlisted in the army 1964 at the age of twenty-one and spent three years touring; one year was in Korea as a US army engineer.

Duane is married and has three children. He started his own company in the Minnesota farming area selling and delivering concrete. Duane was a scoutmaster, a survival expert, and is skilled at living and thriving under some of the most extreme conditions known to man.

He is also a public speaker, who gives presentations on rural living, homesteading, survival, Alaskan living, and interesting topics such as the art of dowsing. Duane moved to Alaska on a whim nearly thirty years ago, after surviving a shot in the head. He and his wife Rena became the last persons to have filed a claim under the Federal Homestead Act of 1862. The Homestead Act of 1862 ended for good in October 1986.

Duane found his second wife through the mail-order bride system and married Rena of Hamilton, Ontario, Canada. Rena moved to the Alaskan homestead to live in a hole in the ground, called a dug out, for nine years while she and Duane built their three-story log home.

They live off the land for the most part, by gardening, using solar power, and trapping. Rena does the skinning. Duane has so named their heaven on earth Ose Mountain and is referred to as Ose Mountain by most.

Duane has now taken to writing and has plans for several books to write while living in their log home on top of Ose Mountain, Alaska. Rena will have a book out on *Wild Game Cooking and Preparation.*

One thing Duane wrote while living in the dugout one winter day is titled *River Days Past.* A TV interview of Duane and Rena Ose on Ose Mountain, completed in 2010, can be viewed on this link: https://www.youtube.com/watch?v=4uurXp8aOps